YOUR FIRST KICKSTARTER CAMPAIGN

VILIUS STANISLOVAITIS

Copyright © 2019 by Vilius Stanislovaitis

All Rights Reserved

No part of this book may be reproduced in any form by any means without the express permission of the author. This includes reprints, excerpts, photocopying, recording, or any future means of reproducing text. If you would like to do any of the above, please seek permission first by sending an email to vilius.stanislovaitis@gmail.com

ISBN: 9781690084129

DOWNLOAD FREE BONUS

150+ USEFUL TOOLS
TO MAXIMISE YOUR
KICKSTARTER CAMPAIGN

Just to say thanks for reading my book,

I would like to give you this Free Bonus!

DOWNLOAD YOUR BONUS HERE:

https://www.kickstarterbook.com/#bonus

TABLE OF CONTENTS

Introduction 1
The Basics of Crowdfunding 5
The Most Funded Kickstarter Campaigns 13
The Craziest Kickstarter Campaigns 17
Platforms: Kickstarter or Indiegogo? 23

    Funding Type 24
    Eligible Countries 26
    The Platform's Fees 27
    Visitor Traffic and Popularity 28
    Categories 30
    The Project Evaluation Standards 32
    Tracking and Remarketing Capabilities 33
    Support 36
    Other Differences 37
    Conclusions 39

Start From an Idea 43

    Find a Large Problem 43
    Create a Prototype 46
    User Behavior and A/B Testing 48
    Building a Team 50

Pre-Launch 55

    Set Your Goal 55
    Analyze Similar Campaigns 59
    Target Audience 73
    Gather Your Crowd (Free Methods) 75
    Landing Page 97
    "Warm Up" Leads 113
    Involve Your Audience 119
    Facebook Ads 121
    Smoke Testing 129
    Pre-Launch Funnel 130
    Conversion Rates 133

Media Outreach 139
Influencers 164
Viral Videos 174
Wrap Up and Action Plan 179

Starting a Project 187

Step 1: Your Eligibility and Project Rules 188
Step 2: Project Image, Title, and Funding Goal 197
Step 3: Project Video 200
Step 4: Project Description 202
Step 5: Rewards and Shipping Costs 204
Step 6: Project Preview 211
Wrap-up and Action Plan 212

Launching and Running the Campaign 215

Project Launch Timing 217
The Launch Day 220
Prepare to Refuse Offers 222
Communication with Backers 223
Stretch Goals 227
Get Traffic from Kickstarter 229
Last Days of Your Project 238
Wrap-up and Action Plan 240

Fulfillment 245

Taxes 246
Survey 246
Communication with Your Backers 247
Amazon Launchpad 249
What if Funding Is Unsuccessful? 249

Final Points 251

Acknowledgements 255

INTRODUCTION

Raising money on Kickstarter looks totally different now to how it did a decade ago, when the platform had just opened in 2009. Crazy ideas such as donating money to hire a man in a plane to write stupid things with clouds in the sky (Kurt Braunohler's Cloud Project) or asking for $10 to make a potato salad which suddenly turns into $55,000 (the Potato Salad project) are hardly possible now. The number of new projects is huge, competition is tight, and you'll barely find an idea which raises more than $100,000 without spending money on advertising.

Exponential growth of the platform has attracted many marketing agencies and individuals. Once you click the "launch" button on Kickstarter, you'll start getting a bunch of offers, such as "I will promote your Kickstarter campaign to 200,000 people in social networks for just $20." Smart marketing specialists who target new, inexperienced project creators have established processes that automatically send highly personalized messages once a new project appears on Kickstarter. Usually, such emails begin with your name and follow with the line, "Your project is really amazing." Well, we all have *ego* and we like when people use our name and say nice words about us or the work we do. The sad truth is that none of these guys will be able to make an impact on your project success.

You'll have to learn to ignore such messages. This will help you focus on your *pre-launch strategy,* which determines if your project is successful or not. Ask any creator who has successfully funded their project on Kickstarter and they will confirm that *pre-launch* is the key to success. This book will explain to you the basics of crowdfunding, but its main focus is to teach you **how to collect potential backers early, in advance, and to make sure you raise at least 30% funding within 48 hours.** Research done by Planting Justice shows that over 90% of Kickstarter campaigns that got 30% funded within 48 hours get fully funded.

When I launched my first Kickstarter project (my book *How to Start a VoIP Business*), I received many offers from strangers who were willing to help. I ignored them all because I knew that my target audience was very niche and all traditional marketing channels just wouldn't work. During the pre-launch phase, I collected around 2000 leads who were informed about my project and waiting for its launch. This list helped me to get fully funded within 5 days and by the end of the campaign, I raised 243% of my initial goal.

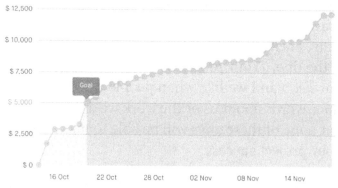

Fig. 1. Funding progress of the book
How to Start a VoIP Business on Kickstarter

After this experience, I got really excited about Kickstarter and interviewed more than 30 Kickstarter project creators from different fields. I wanted to learn their mistakes, tips, dos, don'ts, and key factors to success so that I could share this knowledge with others. Moreover, I participated in a few additional projects as a collaborator, which helped me to practice what I've learned.

I trust that the creator of the idea (yes, you!) can prepare for a Kickstarter launch more efficiently than anyone else on Earth. *You* are the person who is the most motivated to achieve success for your project, and because of this, *you* should have total control of *your* campaign pre-launch. Trust me, it's not rocket science and every person can do this well. In this book, I'll explain how to prepare for your Kickstarter campaign and how to get a crowd of people excited about your project even before it's launched.

In this book I'll mention a lot of useful tools which can automate manual tasks and help you manage other important aspects of preparation for your Kickstarter campaign. Technology changes and because of this some of the tools, described in this book may disappear and new better ones appear. You can get the most recently updated list of 150+ useful tools here: https://www.kickstarterbook.com/#bonus.

THE BASICS OF CROWDFUNDING

There are lots of crowdfunding platforms in the world, but in the category of reward-based crowdfunding, there are two leaders: Kickstarter and Indiegogo. In this book, we are going to talk mainly about Kickstarter because it is the market leader, based on total website visits per month. However, all advice found in the book will be useful for launching your project on any other platform and even presenting a *self-starter* project through your own site, because the main principles of preparation are similar in all cases.

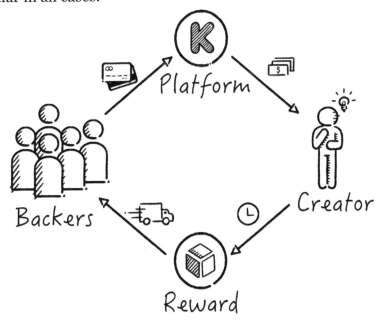

Fig. 2. Crowdfunding diagram

Platform

A crowdfunding platform is a virtual space, where project creators and backers meet. Here, creators get an opportunity to see the demand of their ideas in the global market, to attract their first clients and to raise money for the development of the product. Backers come here to support a certain project, or they just browse to see if there are any new ideas in a category that interests them. People who are ready to support a project can do it without any reward, by donating a small amount or by selecting a certain reward.

Rewards

A reward is what the creator promises to deliver to the backer in exchange for making a pledge (paying a specific amount of money). Rewards can range from a simple "thank you" to a final version of the crowdfunded product (book, movie, game, toy, apparel or anything else that the creator presents in their project). Some project creators add various accessories related to the project as rewards: T-shirts, mugs, stickers, badges, etc. Backers that provide the biggest financial support get to enjoy exclusive privileges—for example, a dinner with the creator and their team, a tour around the workshops where the product was being created, or some other exclusive experience related to the product.

Creators and Backers

From first glance, it may seem that the relationship between creator and backer is a bit like the one between buyer and seller, but there are a couple of essential differences.

Since the purpose of crowdfunding platforms is to make creative ideas a reality, by supporting a project, backers are, in a sense, helping the author to fulfill a dream to create something new and unique. So, by making a pledge, the backer shows their support to what the creator is doing.

The trust between the creator and backer plays a huge role. Trustworthiness is an essential factor creator need to have when asking for pledges. Crowdfunding expert Harry Cutler-Smith, who has reviewed this book, ran an experiment with a focus group and found that the two main factors which impact *backers' motivation to support a project are the key interest and the level of trust in the creator.*

Do backers trust new creators? Not as they used to. Even though the number of Kickstarter backers increased significantly, but due to the failed projects, delays with product delivery and other negative experiences backer confidence has been lost and new creators must try harder than before. On the other hand, if a creator has a group of people who already trust him, that's a huge advantage when preparing for a Kickstarter campaign.

No less important is getting a valuable reward in return. Every backer, after having read the benefits of the project, can roughly estimate their perceived value. If it is higher than the cost of the reward and the backer doesn't know better alternatives and has no further objections, they can make a pledge for the project.

Unlike shopping online, by making a pledge on a crowdfunding platform, the backer agrees to receive a product only after a certain time, which is called the *estimated delivery date*. The delivery date is specified in the description of the reward. The project creator usually calculates it preliminarily, and in reality, backers may have to wait for the product much longer than expected. The creator cannot estimate all circumstances in advance, so it often happens that projects are late. It is a fairly usual occurrence on crowdfunding platforms, so the backers have to get used to it, and creators have to be open and sincere when explaining what has happened, why they are late, and what will be done in an attempt to solve the problems.

Communicating honestly helps create stronger relationships, so the backers are more lenient when the creator is late because the basis of supporting a project is not just to purchase a product, but also to help fulfill the creator's dream. This aspect is not present in normal buyer and seller relationships, which are regulated and have stricter rules than the freer creator and backer relationships.

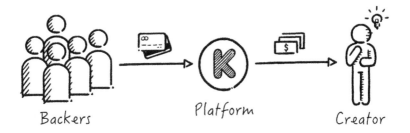

Fig. 3. Crowdfunding participants.

Crowdfunding Myths

Some people, after having read crowdfunding success stories in the press, scratch their heads and think "Everything is simple: I should upload the video, describe the idea, and I'll get some money." They seem to think that the platform itself will find the backers or maybe that creators of successful projects will reveal their "secret trick" for getting financed. Unfortunately, that is just a myth—which some people believe in without having delved into the subtleties of crowdfunding.

Ideas that are presented on a crowdfunding platform without any additional preparation quickly disappear in the midst of thousands of other projects, which compete for users' attention in their categories. Every platform has its own internal algorithms but the gist of them is that the projects that attract new backers and raise funding faster than others will appear higher in the platform's search results. That's why you'll have to understand what your potential backers look like, where to find them, and how to gauge their interest before starting the campaign.

Projects

Every rewards-based crowdfunding platform has its own rules, project categories, and prohibited items. But in general, most projects are united by the fact that they are creative and innovative. They could be movies, books, music, games, technological or design projects, but the ideas have to be new, exceptional, and unique in one way or another.

When presenting a project, the creator has to set funding goals and a campaign duration. To realize small personal projects, it's enough to raise a few hundred dollars, while technological projects with mass production may need hundreds of thousands of dollars.

Platforms and the Creator's Responsibility

Most rewards-based crowdfunding platforms operate on a system of trust, and backers ultimately decide the validity of a project. The creator is responsible for completing the project and shipping rewards to their backers.

If the creator is late to deliver the product, they will not receive a penalty from the crowdfunding platform, but their backers will start to worry, become upset, and may share negative feedback publicly. This can damage project's brand and creator's reputation. That's why personal responsibility and trust are the key elements in the creator and backers' relationship.

The platform itself takes no responsibility and the backers themselves have to decide the worthiness of a project by supporting it or not. However, this does not mean that the platform will not do anything. Kickstarter reviews projects before they are allowed to launch to make sure they don't include prohibited items and meet the platform's rules. According to Kickstarter statistics, they accept about 80% of the projects that come their way.

THE MOST FUNDED KICKSTARTER CAMPAIGNS

The first and third places on Kickstarter by funds raised belong to the well-known smartwatch company Pebble, which organized three (two of them were record-breaking) campaigns on Kickstarter.

The history of the company started in 2012 when the first Pebble smartwatch was presented on Kickstarter. It was unique with its brave design and e-paper screen, which is more visible in bright light and consumes less energy. It is worth mentioning that in those days, the smartwatch market was rather empty.

Pebble then broke all records and collected more than $10 million. The company sold a million watches by the end of 2014. In 2015, they broke their original record on Kickstarter by collecting almost twice as much—$20 338 986. To date, it is still the largest sum collected on the Kickstarter and Indiegogo platforms. Unfortunately, in 2016, Pebble officially announced that they were shutting down because of financial difficulties.

Fig. 4. Pebble Time raised $20,338,986 on Kickstarter (photo from their Kickstarter campaign page)

The second most funded campaign on the Kickstarter is the Coolest Cooler. It broke the first Pebble record and raised over $13 million, making it the most funded Kickstarter campaign of 2014. The Coolest Cooler is a multifunction cooler for those who enjoy being outdoors: camping, tailgating, boating, beach parties, picnics, barbecues, etc. The cooler has features like an ice-crushing blender, a USB charging port, LED lamps, a Bluetooth water-resistant speaker, a bottle opener, a knife, plates, a corkscrew, and much more.

The interesting fact is that this was the second attempt for the product's creator Ryan Grepper on Kickstarter. The first campaign was launched on Kickstarter in November 2013 and failed to meet its $150,000 goal. According to the project author, after this campaign he learned the essential mistakes he'd made: the goal set was too large, the design of the product was unfinished and the season was probably not the most appropriate.

Seven months later, Ryan Grepper organized the second Coolest Cooler campaign. This time, the product was more complete, it was a more appropriate season for coolers—the height of summer was chosen—and backers from the first campaign were really active and supportive.

After the previous failure, the author's expectations were lower, but what happened in the first two days was positively shocking. In less than 36 hours, $50 thousand was raised and after another day, the million-dollar mark was reached! The sum continued growing, because the news spread in the media and attracted new backers.

Fig. 5. Coolest Cooler raised $13,285,226 on Kickstarter
(photo from their Kickstarter campaign page)

Sometimes, we all dream about raising millions, but we don't estimate that with great success comes huge responsibility. The authors of the above-mentioned projects encountered difficulties when the time came to meet their obligations and deliver rewards for backers.

Creators of the most funded Kickstarter campaigns had never worked on projects of such a scale, so being late was quite understandable. Unlike those who peacefully create something in their garage, the people who receive a large amount of funding through crowdfunding will experience constant pressure from the backers waiting for the promised product and the media that watches their every move through a magnifying glass.

THE CRAZIEST KICKSTARTER CAMPAIGNS

We've talked seriously, but now let's move to more fun topics. Kickstarter's slogan emphasizes that it is the largest crowdfunding platform which helps to realize *creative ideas*. Some of those ideas are really innovative and great, some are average, and some are completely insane. The Internet loves weird and funny stories and as a result, some most bizarre projects are brought to life. Here are a few of the craziest Kickstarter projects that have been fully funded.

Potato Salad

The Potato Salad project on Kickstarter has garnered perhaps the most attention worldwide. You may be wondering what is so unusual about this salad. Frankly speaking, nothing special. Zack "Danger" Brown, the author of this project, just wanted to make a potato salad, and asked for $10. By the way, this is a good lesson for those who think only about big goals—sometimes it's good idea to start small.

Then the unexpected happened. Some seemed to love the simplicity of this idea and some thought it was a really great joke. Whatever the reason, news about this project went viral and started quickly spreading on social media and in the press. Zack decided to create a stretch goal, where he promised to create a potato salad party where more than a thousand people could gather and everyone would get at least a bite of the potato salad. In the end, the project was backed by almost 7,000 backers who pledged $55,492.

Fig. 6. The Potato Salad project
(photo from their Kickstarter campaign page)

Writing Stupid Things in the Sky

Probably everyone has seen movies where an airplane spells out names, slogans, or short phrases in the sky. This might have inspired Kurt Braunohler, who decided to organize a campaign on Kickstarter by announcing that his idea was to hire a person who would write stupid things in the sky. He asked to help him pull off this incredibly idiotic stunt and he achieved his goal successfully. There were 257 like-minded people who pledged $6,820 to bring Kurt's project to life. Based on backers' votes, it was decided to write "How do I land?" in the clouds.

Fig. 7. Kurt Braunohler's Notes in the Sky
(photo from their Kickstarter campaign page)

Giant Inflatable Sculpture of Lionel Richie's Head

Many have bands or artists they like. Some worship them more, some less, and the rest are ready to perform insane tasks for their idols. We can attribute a group of Lionel Richie fans from Spain to this category. They decided to create a gigantic inflatable head of Lionel Richie and went to look for funding on the Kickstarter. The idea was supported by 211 backers, who donated more £8,000. A super-sized version of Lionel Richie's head was unveiled at the music festival Bestival.

Fig. 8. Inflatable head of Lionel Richie
(photo from their Kickstarter campaign page)

Grizzly Coat

There are many authors who try hard to analyze the market and understand the needs of their target audience, in order to present practical and innovative ideas on crowdfunding platforms. And then, among all those practical projects, this really weird Kickstarter campaign catches your eye... a faux-fur grizzly bear jacket! The Griz Coat project was created by three young guys and they raised almost $30,000! In such cases, you can only be surprised: "What...? How...?"

The authors of this idea proved that demand for a synthetic leather bear coat with teeth-decorated headgear actually exists. Who could have known? This campaign was even marked as the project of the week on Kickstarter. This story shows that even the craziest ideas can be funded.

Fig. 9. Grizzly coat (photo from their Kickstarter campaign page)

IllumiBowl Toilet Night Light

This was not only a crazy project, but also the most funded of all the weird projects I've mentioned here. IllumiBowl is a motion-activated night light that sets to any single color or color-rotate. It can be clipped onto the side of your toilet, and lights up your toilet bowl in one of eight colors.

What's interesting is that the project video was super-simple and funny. The creators even included a value-proposition for boys: "No more aiming in the dark" and girls: "No more falling in." The campaign slogan was "Pee happy. Pee safe. Pee free." Media really liked this story and IllumiBowl was featured in Engadget, Gizmodo, CNET, Tech Void, OhGizmo!, etc.

The initial goal of this project was $20,000 but it

ended up raising over $95,399! After three years, the IllumiBowl team came back to Kickstarter with an improved version of their product and raised even more than the first time: $105,280!

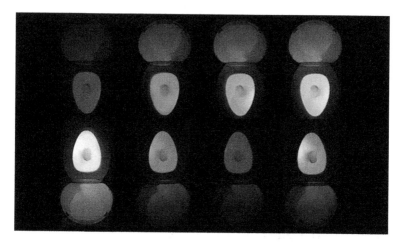

Fig. 10. IllumiBowl Toilet Night Light
(photo from their Kickstarter campaign page)

PLATFORMS: KICKSTARTER OR INDIEGOGO?

The public statistics on the Kickstarter site show that through this platform, $4 billion has been raised from more than 16 million backers, who have helped to realize more than 167,000 projects. I am certain that when you are reading this book the numbers will have increased. The average project success rate is 37.18%.

In general, revealing numbers is a good thing because it shows transparency, which increases the platform's credibility. Meanwhile, Indiegogo doesn't publish such detailed statistics on their website, but they do have some numbers on their site:

- 10 million people visit their website each month.
- 9 million backers helped bring more than 800,000 innovative ideas to life.
- ~19,000 campaigns are launched every month.

I didn't find stats about new campaigns on Kickstarter, but I would say that Indiegogo has an impressive number. However, even if Indiegogo has more new campaigns than Kickstarter, there's something you should know. Kickstarter has a stricter policy for new projects and as a result, they accept only 80% of projects that submit their applications. What choice do creators have if they cannot meet Kickstarter's requirements or if their project is rejected by the platform? They go to Indiegogo which is more open. It's great that an alternative for such creators exists, but on the other hand, this leads to lower-quality projects in Indiegogo.

So, what to choose: Kickstarter or Indiegogo? Let's examine the differences between these two platforms and at the end of this chapter, I'll give you some final thoughts that will help you to make a decision.

FUNDING TYPE

The Kickstarter platform uses *all-or-nothing* funding. This means that backers will not be charged for their pledges unless the project reaches its funding goal. Indiegogo is more flexible in this aspect because it allows choosing both *fixed* or *flexible* funding. Flexible funding allows you to keep all your funds, even when your campaign doesn't reach its goal. Fixed funding is similar to Kickstarter's all-or-nothing approach. The main difference is that if the funding goal isn't reached, Kickstarter backers won't be charged for the amount they pledged and Indiegogo backers will be refunded by the platform within 5–7 business days.

Choosing a funding type depends on what you create. If you create a personal project, where any amount you raise is useful and you plan to realize your idea anyway, you can choose flexible funding. Suppose you have written a book and are asking for $3000 to publish it. If you don't raise $3000, would you refuse to publish the book, into which you've put your heart and soul? I don't think so. I'm sure that even partial funding would be worthwhile.

On the other hand, there are many projects (hardware, technology, design, etc.) that require manufacturing in order to produce the first batch of products. Usually, there's some minimum order quantity so the price of your product can be competitive. The higher volume of units you produce, the higher profit margin you get, or the lower rate per unit you can offer. When setting a fixed goal, you should consider the least amount you need to raise, so the fulfillment on your product with this minimum order quantity is possible. If you don't achieve this goal, such a project is not worth starting because you will either not make any profit or will experience losses. A fixed goal is very clear and motivating in most cases.

It is important to mention that both platforms allow exceeding the primary goal. For example, the Potato Salad project set a goal of $10, but raised $55,492. It's always better to set a smaller goal rather than a bigger goal, unless you are sure that if you do not reach the necessary goal, you will not be able to further develop the project. The higher the goal you choose, the more resources you will need to realize it and the longer and more difficult the work will be. The psychological factor is important as well because there will always be a category of potential backers who will not back the project until it reaches 100% of the set goal. Immediately after the campaign reaches full funding, project's value in the eyes of the backers increases, and they will gladly make a pledge with a steady hand.

ELIGIBLE COUNTRIES

Project creation on Kickstarter is currently available to permanent residents in the US, UK, Canada, Australia, New Zealand, the Netherlands, Denmark, Ireland, Norway, Sweden, Germany, France, Spain, Italy, Austria, Belgium, Switzerland, Luxembourg, Hong Kong, Singapore, Mexico, and Japan.

Previously Indiegogo allowed anyone in the world to start a campaign as long as they had a bank account. But recently they have updated their policy. Now Indiegogo campaign creation is currently available to individuals in the US, UK, Canada, Australia, Hong Kong (China campaigns may be eligible), Austria, Belgium, Denmark, Germany, Finland, France, Republic of Ireland, Italy, Luxembourg, Netherlands, Norway, Portugal, Singapore, Spain, Sweden, or Switzerland.

If you're outside eligible countries, it's still possible to launch the project. You just need to get a bank account in one of those countries, or ask a partner or friend from an eligible country to assist you with account registration. I did this myself and I'll explain everything in more detail in the chapter "Starting a Project." Just keep in mind that this is against platform's policy, so if you don't want to take risks and get involved with workarounds, simply choose another platform.

THE PLATFORM'S FEES

Kickstarter and Indiegogo have the same 5% platform fee on all funds raised for your campaign. In addition to this, there's around 3-5% payment-processing fee (both platforms use Stripe for credit card processing). There may also be an additional wire transfer fee, depending on your currency and bank account location.

Even though platforms use the same payment partner (Stripe), their payment processing policy is different. Indiegogo processes credit cards immediately after the pledge is done and Kickstarter starts payment processing only after the project is successfully finished. This means that when the backer makes a pledge on Kickstarter, the platform just saves the credit card data, but does not deduct the money. The actual charge is done after the campaign ends and if the funding goal is reached.

It often happens that due to various reasons, Stripe is not able to deduct money from some credit cards. In such cases, backers with errored pledges have one week to update their credit cards. These backers get a few reminders and after a week has passed, Kickstarter attempts to collect their pledges automatically for the last time. If attempt is unsuccessful, such pledges are dropped.

I didn't find any objective statistics of what percentage of payments remain unprocessed, but you should emotionally be prepared to lose up to 10%. This percentage can be lower or higher, but what really matters is how this affects your funding goal. In my first project, I lost about 5% of my funding goal. I contacted backers with errored pledges privately and suggested they pay by PayPal. But in the last project I participated in, we lost 17% of the total funding due to dropped pledges! To tell you the truth, I didn't expect to lose such an amount, but be aware that this can happen.

What we've discussed here are *dropped pledges* (unsuccessful attempts to process the backer's credit card), but you'll also have some *canceled pledges* if some backers change their mind during the campaign and decide to cancel their pledge. For that reason, it's important to message backers immediately after they make a pledge because in this case, your communication is saved and you'll be able to message them again and have a chance to bring them back. If you don't do this and they cancel their pledge, you will no longer be able to contact such backers through Kickstarter again.

VISITOR TRAFFIC AND POPULARITY

In terms of visitor traffic and popularity, Kickstarter significantly outstrips its closest competitor. In this section, we'll use three tools to compare these two crowdfunding platforms: SimilarWeb for website traffic volume, Google Trends for the number of search queries in Google Search, and Audience Insights for popularity on Facebook.

According to similarweb.com, which provides web analytics services and shows the website traffic volume, referral sources, and other useful information, the visitor traffic on Kickstarter is much larger than on Indiegogo.

However, there were two months when Indiegogo had more total visits than Kickstarter. Even though it was rather an exception, there's a chance that statistics will change in the future.

There's an interesting fact—Indiegogo gets some traffic from referrals (websites that are sending traffic to them directly) and Kickstarter is the top referring site. This happens because Indiegogo accepts projects that are successfully funded on Kickstarter and allows them to continue pre-orders on Indiegogo through the InDemand program (we'll discuss this possibility later in this book).

If you check referrals for Kickstarter, you'll find out that the top referring site is jellopads.com. It belongs to Jellop Crowdfunding, which is a small team of crowdfunding professionals who focus on Kickstarter projects that are trending toward $200,000 or more.

Another way to compare platforms is by using Google Trends, which analyzes the popularity of top search queries in Google Search across various regions and languages. If you compare the number of searches of the keywords "Kickstarter" and "Indiegogo" at trends.google.com, you will see that the interest in the keyword "Kickstarter" is much higher than "Indiegogo."

The last tool is Audience Insights, where you can see how many Facebook users have a particular interest. Audience Insights does not allow comparing interests worldwide and you must choose a certain country, region, or city. Both Kickstarter and Indiegogo get most traffic from the United States, so I have chosen users from this country for comparison. There are 9–10 million monthly active Facebook users with an interest in "Kickstarter" and 3.5–4 million with an interest in "Indiegogo" in the United States, so Kickstarter is a clear winner here too.

Kickstarter is way ahead in popularity compared to Indiegogo, but does it have an influence on your project's funding? Will at least a small part of the platform's visitors become your backers? In order to convert Kickstarter's visitors to backers, there are two options (we'll review them in more detail later in this book): to be mentioned in the platform's communication channels (newsletter, social media or blog) or to appear higher in the platform's search.

Kickstarter has a dedicated team that reviews new projects, selects exceptional ones, and marks them as "Projects We Love." Such projects then appear higher in the platform's default search and few of them are mentioned in the newsletter and social networks. As a result, such projects get an additional stream of visitors and some of them may convert to backers. Another option is to become a *trending* project, to appear higher in your project's category.

CATEGORIES

There are 15 project categories on Kickstarter: Art, Comics, Crafts, Dance, Design, Fashion, Film & Video, Food, Games, Journalism, Music, Photography, Publishing,

Technology, and Theater. Most campaigns are in the movie, video, music, and publishing categories, while the largest sums have been donated to the game, design, and technology categories. Each category has a few subcategories. Overall, you can create and discover projects in 94 subcategories.

Indiegogo was initially dedicated to the funding of independent movies, but the category list on the site was quickly expanded to accommodate a variety of crowdfunding campaigns. Now they have the following categories:

1. **TECH & INNOVATION.** Audio, Camera Gear, Energy & Green Tech, Fashion & Wearables, Food & Beverages, Health & Fitness, Home, Phones & Accessories, Productivity, Transportation, Travel & Outdoors, Other Innovative Products.
2. **CREATIVE WORKS.** Art, Comics, Dance & Theater, Film, Music, Photography, Podcasts, Blogs & Vlogs, Tabletop Games, Video Games, Web Series & TV Shows, Writing & Publishing, Other Creations.
3. **COMMUNITY PROJECTS.** Animal Rights, Culture, Education, Environment, Human Rights, Local Businesses, Spirituality, Wellness, Other Community Projects.

It's important to note that categories and subcategories are constantly updated, depending on market situations and new projects. If you have an idea that you plan to launch, check if there are similar successfully funded projects on Kickstarter or Indiegogo. You can then talk to the creators of those projects and ask why they decided to choose that platform.

THE PROJECT EVALUATION STANDARDS

Kickstarter has higher project standards and stricter evaluation criteria than Indiegogo. Kickstarter requires backers to show a prototype without using "photorealistic renderings" to start a campaign, has a list of requirements for creators, and rules for their projects (we'll review them later in this book).

The project review process may take 2–3 business days and about 80% of the submitted projects are accepted. This results in higher quality campaigns and gives more confidence for backers. Of course, no one is protected 100%, but history shows that if the Kickstarter team thinks you're trying to scam backers, they'll shut your project down. There are actually some projects on Kickstarter that reached significant funding and were suspended due to various reasons. Some of those projects then moved to Indiegogo and were accepted.

Indiegogo, on the other hand, does not require any working prototype. You just have to submit the necessary information and you can present your project without any special review processes. This means that you shouldn't worry if your project will be accepted or not and you can launch your campaign much faster.

There's one story I have related to higher project

evaluation standards. Ignas was one of the creators I interviewed whose project wasn't accepted on Kickstarter and was then launched on Indiegogo. His first campaign, the colorful, minimalistic Pigeon kick scooter, was successfully funded on Kickstarter, so after two years he decided to launch another project: Raven, the lightest and most compact foldable scooter, made from carbon fiber material.

After submitting the Raven project to Kickstarter, it wasn't accepted because the project images were considered to be "photorealistic renderings of a product concept." Kickstarter asked him to remove all images that were eye-catching and add simpler photos of a prototype, so backers would clearly see that this was something new, still in the prototype stage. But even though Ignas had a prototype, he didn't understand why he should put lower quality photos when he could show more attractive photos that represent his product very well. He got a bit angry because of this policy and decided to launch his campaign on Indiegogo. Unfortunately, the campaign wasn't successful and Ignas thought that his decision to change platform might have been one of his mistakes. "Kickstarter has stricter policies, but they still have a much bigger audience," said Ignas.

TRACKING AND REMARKETING CAPABILITIES

Indiegogo allows using a public API, giving you real-time backer information, and offers a built-in analytics platform where you can monitor activity with a conversion pixel. With that pixel in place, you can do remarketing for the visitors of your campaign page, which can lead to additional conversions. Indiegogo also gives you access to backers' email addresses while you're live. This gives you the possibility to create lookalike audiences of these backers and target them via Facebook ads.

Kickstarter offers the possibility to insert a Google Analytics tracking ID and there's a feature called Custom Referral Tags which allows you to create custom links and track if someone backed the project using this link. In Table 1, you can see how this information is displayed in the Creator Dashboard.

Referrers that have the type "Custom" were generated using Custom Referral Tags. In this particular case, we generated tracking links for our mailing list ("email_leads"), media outreach list ("Press&Blogs"), an email reminder that we sent 23 hours before the end of the project ("23 hours left"), and Facebook ads ("Facebook Ads"), etc. By using this functionality, we could evaluate the efficiency of our marketing strategies.

Referrer	Type	# of Pledges	% of Pledged	Pledged
email_leads	Custom	13	22.51%	£3,135
Direct traffic no referrer information	External	12	19.65%	£2,736
Search	Kickstarter	9	14.76%	£2,056
Facebook	External	4	7.22%	£1,005

Advanced Discovery	Kickstarter	4	5.59%	£779
google.com	External	2	4.63%	£645
Press&Blogs	Custom	3	3.63%	£505
23 hours left	Custom	1	2.15%	£300
Facebook Ads	Custom	1	2.15%	£300

Table 1. Referrers functionality on Kickstarter

Even though Custom Referral Tags is a great tool, it lacks accuracy. As you see in Table 1, 19.65% of pledges came from "Direct traffic no referrer information," 14.76% from Kickstarter Search, 7.22% from Facebook, and 4.63% from Google. What does that tell us? There's a big chance that these backers belong to our mailing list, follow us on Facebook, or have heard about us from some other marketing channel we've used, but they decided not to make a pledge immediately. Instead, they waited for some time, then remembered us (or saw our ad) and searched for our project later on Facebook, Google, or Kickstarter. As a result, we cannot track the path of their actions and more than a half of traffic is unaccounted for.

To summarize, the tracking and remarketing capabilities of Kickstarter are still far from the Indiegogo. A big drawback is that Kickstarter doesn't allow you to insert a pixel, so you won't be able to retarget visitors that come to the campaign page. But on the other hand, not displaying backers' emails and not allowing a pixel means that Kickstarter does a better job in terms of user privacy policy. As a result, this gives more confidence to backers to support projects on Kickstarter.

SUPPORT

This area is hard to evaluate because the opinions are fairly varied. While writing this book, I read a lot of reviews saying that the support on Indiegogo is stronger, but after having talked to other project creators, I heard different opinions.

I can only say that the support on Kickstarter did not impress me. I expected faster response times because like all project creators, I was in hurry. But taking into consideration that there are three-four thousand active projects on Kickstarter and many authors are trying their luck for the first time, the response time is reasonable. After a while, I began to understand when their support team started work and when queries should be sent to receive an answer quickly.

Another thing which I didn't like was that support representatives always pointed me to the FAQ, which I'd already read before contacting them. But then I learned how to communicate more efficiently with them and since then, I've started all new support requests by saying, "I've read this FAQ, but I still have a question..." This helped to save some time. But overall, most processes are automated and usually you need some help before registering your campaign and after the campaign is finished.

OTHER DIFFERENCES

There are several additional differences between the platforms, but I do not think that they are essential or could influence your final choice.

Video Hosting

Indiegogo videos must be uploaded on either the YouTube or Vimeo platform. Kickstarter has its own video hosting, which means that you don't have to worry about creating additional accounts just to upload your project's video. On the other hand, YouTube is the second largest search system and could work as an additional marketing tool that would help attract potential backers. But I wouldn't give a plus for Indiegogo for that, because you can upload a video to YouTube yourself, even if you present a campaign on the Kickstarter platform. By simply uploading the video to YouTube, you won't get noticed—unless your clip gets a lot of views and shares in a short time.

Rewards (Perks)

Something that you offer to backers in exchange for their support is called a "reward" on Kickstarter or a "perk" on Indiegogo. Indiegogo gives more flexibility here. You can choose a Featured Perk, which a good way to highlight your campaign's most popular perk (you can change the perk you have listed at any time). Then there's the Secret Perk that is only available for visitors via a unique link that you distribute. This could be a perfect tool for target audience segmentation and when creating special conditions for more loyal backers (e.g. those who registered in advance). In terms of tracking, a Secret Perk is more effective than Custom Referral Tags on Kickstarter. Custom Referral Tags just point potential backers to the campaign page, and they are not motivated to support a project immediately and specifically through that link, whereas a Secret Perk gives a strong motive to support a project through this unique link because the backer will get something exclusive.

Preorders

Indiegogo offers an excellent opportunity to create an InDemand page and continue raising money after the campaign officially ends and reaches its goal. This means that Indiegogo can be used as a simple e-commerce store for collecting preorders.

You can also launch an InDemand page on Indiegogo after your Kickstarter campaign is finished. In this case, Indiegogo shows the amount that you've already raised on Kickstarter and allows you to continue preorders. This is a great option because you already have all the needed material: video, visualizations, description, and rewards, so it will not take much time to just copy-paste it. Also by launching an InDemand project, you'll be temporarily exposed to Indiegogo's audience.

Using the InDemand program, project creators I've interviewed raised extra funding in Indiegogo with minimal effort. The vertical bicycle parking system PARKIS raised an additional $46,467 while a smart smoothie maker called Millo raised an additional $18,323. The platform fee in InDemand is 5% if you ran your campaign on Indiegogo, or 8% if you ran your campaign on Kickstarter. The InDemand page gives the creator some time to build an e-commerce website without losing the opportunity to generate pre-orders.

CONCLUSIONS

I believe that there will be even more differences in the future as both the Kickstarter and Indiegogo platforms are quickly becoming more adaptive, improving their services, and are watching out for competitors. Here are a few final points about the platforms:

1. The platform itself does not guarantee any success. Whatever platform you choose, you will still have to attract your target audience in advance, engage with them, and keep driving traffic to your project throughout the campaign.
2. Look for similar projects on both platforms. Analyze these projects and talk to their authors. This study will allow you to reach a much more rational decision than just reading comparisons between the platforms.
3. Do you already have a sufficient number of potential backers (whether they are your friends, acquaintances, followers, clients, potential clients, partners, etc.)? If so, it will not matter what platform you choose. You can even raise money directly through your own site.
4. Are from a country that is not supported by Kickstarter or Indiegogo? In this book, I'll tell you few workarounds to use so you can get accepted. But

if you don't want to go to the trouble of getting a bank account in an eligible country or asking your friend from a supported country to verify their account, you can simply choose another platform, which supports your country or create your own crowdfunding page with crowdfunding plugins for WordPress.

Despite all the differences, my personal choice (you might have already guessed this by the name of the book) is still Kickstarter. I think the key factor for every creator is to get backers. Even though you have to find them and point them to the campaign yourself, the chance of getting additional backers from the platform are higher if you choose Kickstarter. It is undoubtedly the leader by visitor traffic and popularity.

What I also like is that the Kickstarter platform is very open with sharing their statistics. It seems they have a really strong and loyal community:

- 32% of backers supported more than one project.
- 700,000 backers supported more than 10 projects.
- 27,000 backers supported more than 100 projects.

There's one more thing that plays a big role in choosing a platform: conversion of paid traffic, which determines how far you can scale your campaign. While doing interviews with project creators, I spoke to Adomas Baltagalvis, who has spent over $2 million on Facebook ads to attract new backers to the crowdfunding campaigns of his clients. He was a primary advertiser of some platform fee in InDemand is 5% if you ran your campaign on Indiegogo, or 8% if you ran your campaign on Kickstarter. The InDemand page gives the creator some time to build an e-commerce website without losing the opportunity to generate pre-orders.

CONCLUSIONS

I believe that there will be even more differences in the future as both the Kickstarter and Indiegogo platforms are quickly becoming more adaptive, improving their services, and are watching out for competitors. Here are a few final points about the platforms:

1. The platform itself does not guarantee any success. Whatever platform you choose, you will still have to attract your target audience in advance, engage with them, and keep driving traffic to your project throughout the campaign.
2. Look for similar projects on both platforms. Analyze these projects and talk to their authors. This study will allow you to reach a much more rational decision than just reading comparisons between the platforms.
3. Do you already have a sufficient number of potential backers (whether they are your friends, acquaintances, followers, clients, potential clients, partners, etc.)? If so, it will not matter what platform you choose. You can even raise money directly through your own site.
4. Are from a country that is not supported by Kickstarter or Indiegogo? In this book, I'll tell you few workarounds to use so you can get accepted. But

if you don't want to go to the trouble of getting a bank account in an eligible country or asking your friend from a supported country to verify their account, you can simply choose another platform, which supports your country or create your own crowdfunding page with crowdfunding plugins for WordPress.

Despite all the differences, my personal choice (you might have already guessed this by the name of the book) is still Kickstarter. I think the key factor for every creator is to get backers. Even though you have to find them and point them to the campaign yourself, the chance of getting additional backers from the platform are higher if you choose Kickstarter. It is undoubtedly the leader by visitor traffic and popularity.

What I also like is that the Kickstarter platform is very open with sharing their statistics. It seems they have a really strong and loyal community:

- 32% of backers supported more than one project.
- 700,000 backers supported more than 10 projects.
- 27,000 backers supported more than 100 projects.

There's one more thing that plays a big role in choosing a platform: conversion of paid traffic, which determines how far you can scale your campaign. While doing interviews with project creators, I spoke to Adomas Baltagalvis, who has spent over $2 million on Facebook ads to attract new backers to the crowdfunding campaigns of his clients. He was a primary advertiser of some of the most successful crowdfunding campaigns, including Filippo Loreti (€4.8 million), MyKronoz ($5.3 million), Superscreen ($2.5 million), LIV Watches ($1.7 million and $1.1 million), Quartz Bottle ($1.3 million) and Sequent (1 million CHF), where he put his love for algorithms and data analysis into full action. Most of Adomas' work has been done for Kickstarter projects, but he has also tried to run ads for Indiegogo campaigns. He told me that Facebook advertising for Kickstarter projects had a much higher conversion rate than for Indiegogo campaigns. This caught my attention and I decided to find out more about this.

Funded Today is a marketing agency that spends a lot of money on Facebook and Google advertising for crowdfunding campaigns. On their website, they state that they have helped to raise more than $240 million. That's a significant amount, which shows that they have a lot of useful data, which can help to make certain conclusions in our comparison between Kickstarter and Indiegogo. Thomas Alvord, co-founder of Funded Today, said that "in deciding between Kickstarter vs Indiegogo, the answer is 100% Kickstarter." Thomas has shared some juicy stats on the Funded Today blog, and based on the data that his agency has gathered, he calculated that "looking at campaigns that raise $10,000+, you are 3–5 times more likely to hit that amount on Kickstarter than on Indiegogo." In addition to this, he added that subjectively, their entire team at Funded Today has said for years that "Kickstarter is better than Indiegogo because conversion rates on Indiegogo are always 3–4 times lower." Funded Today states that they "have more data on marketing results than anyone in the world, including even Kickstarter and Indiegogo."

Why does Kickstarter have a better conversion rate than Indiegogo? I can't give an exact answer, but it seems that Kickstarter has a stronger brand and by adding more qualification criteria for projects, they have built a loyal community of backers who trust the platform. So, if you plan to attract backers by running Facebook ads, you should certainly choose Kickstarter.

START FROM AN IDEA

Everything starts from an idea and the idea arises out of your own interests, skill or the passion you have. Or just something you brainstorm or think about for some time. You may also take an existing product and see how you can improve it. There are lots of projects like this and these goes to show that not all great ideas are original. In all those cases, you should find a problem that you will solve.

If the problem is especially relevant to a certain group of people (target audience), and that group is big enough, you may try to create a prototype and collect feedback from your target audience. Based on their reactions, you can decide if it is worth launching a crowdfunding campaign and evaluating the market demand for your idea.

FIND A LARGE PROBLEM

The most successful projects solve the biggest problems. There are a million problems that people have and this creates an infinite supply of business ideas. But what really matters, aside from good timing and a bit of luck, is the execution. You just need to start and focus on one problem that you could help to solve.

First, I would like to tell you what originally encouraged me to write my first book. I was working as a sales manager in a company that was developing telecom billing and routing systems for small telecommunication operators. I have to admit that nearly two years after starting this job, I still hardly understood what the value-added service of our solutions was, and why companies were buying our products. As time passed it became clearer, and I noticed that most of our clients were using our system as their main tool to manage VoIP (voice over IP, also known as Internet telephony) business. They would buy and sell calls on the international wholesale VoIP market, successfully making money from the price difference, and our system allowed them to automate the processes of call setup, accounting, statistics, and reporting. This kind of business seemed interesting to me, so I started looking into what is necessary for creating a successful VoIP business besides the system that we were supplying.

In a couple of months, I collected the necessary information and prepared a ten-page whitepaper called "How to start a calling card business." When I uploaded it on our site, I was surprised: every day the whitepaper was downloaded several dozen times and I received plenty of questions. After browsing the Internet, I noticed that there was no book about VoIP business, so the existing demand and constant questions on that topic inspired me to write the book called "How to Start a VoIP Business" that I later successfully funded on Kickstarter.

My next story is about Bronius Rauba, the creator of the bicycle parking system called PARKIS, that raised €78,505 on Kickstarter. Bronius used to have several bicycles and could only store them on his balcony, so it was important for him to effectively use space. According to the creator of PARKIS, the most effective way to store is to stand the item upright: books on shelves, pencils in a pencil-holder, plates in a cupboard and many other things stand upright.

At the start, he used to hang the bicycles on a hook, but that was difficult—when lifting them, his back would often hurt. Then he understood that the ideal solution should lift the bicycle in the vertical position with minimal physical effort. After having built the first version of the product for himself, friends and relatives encouraged him to present the idea to the world. And that's how PARKIS became reality.

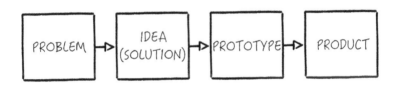

Fig. 11. The path from discerning the problem to the creation of the product

Adam, the creator of Millo, the world's smartest smoothie maker, encountered the problem of being stuck in a low energy loop. His friend, a fitness and nutrition professional, recommended adding workouts and healthy smoothies to Adam's life. At the start, Adam made smoothies with a regular blender, which was very noisy and would wake up his wife and daughter. This encouraged the creator to look into quietly working technologies. Totally unexpectedly, Adam noticed that his daughter's toy was working in an interesting way. Two dancers were spinning on top of the box without any physical attachment to it. Magnets inside the box made them spin. The toy made Adam wonder: could a blender work like that? This was the beginning of quietly working Millo blender that later raised £82,020 on Kickstarter.

Fig. 12. Adam's daughter's toy—a music box with dancers spinning on top of it

Have you ever encountered a problem and thought, "Why has no one solved it yet?" This might be a good start for a new business idea. So, try to notice problems, ask if other people experience them, and propose your solutions. Who knows, maybe it will turn out to a new business opportunity.

CREATE A PROTOTYPE

It's often not enough to have just an idea, which is just a theoretical concept of how a solution should work. That's why creators materialize their ideas and create a prototype that can be presented to the target audience. A *minimal viable product,* or MVP, is a popular development technique, adhering to the principle that you should reject all unnecessary details and create a product or service with as few features as possible, that still satisfies the basic needs of your early customers (early adopters). To those who want to find out more about this method, I recommend reading the Eric Ries book *The Lean Startup*.

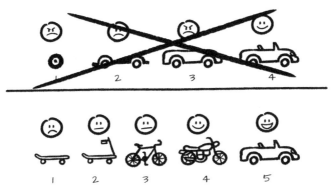

Fig. 13. How (not) to develop a minimal viable product
(illustration idea taken from Henrik Kniberg's blog)

If you want to start a crowdfunding campaign on the Indiegogo platform, a prototype is not necessary, but Kickstarter requires you have it. Thinking from the backers' perspective, it is a reasonable level of entry for new campaigns. Backers are already risking their money by making pledges for something new that has not been developed yet. So, if there's no prototype yet, there's an even higher risk of possible deviations from the initial idea and being late when delivering the final product. Backers tend to support ideas without a prototype less often, and it is much harder for the creator to evaluate all possible costs and the base price of the product.

Every product creator has to establish a connection with the target audience as early as possible, so they can find out their opinions. This is one of the lessons I learned, forgot, and re-learned again while writing my first book. I proved that there's a demand by presenting a 10-page whitepaper, which was my MVP. But then I spent four years writing a book, while separated from the entire world. Only in the last year I understood that this had been a big mistake (thanks to the book *Ape: Author, Publisher, Entrepreneur. How to Publish a Book* by Guy Kawasaki and Shawn Welch), so I included readers into the book writing process again. They could read the draft, add their comments, and vote on the cover of the book. This allowed me to find out reader opinions and improve the manuscript. Besides this, the people who participated in this process became my first supporters once the project was launched on Kickstarter.

I recommend gathering at least 50 people who fit your target audience and who can share their feedback. They will help you in validating the product, improving it, and might be your first backers once your crowdfunding campaign is live.

USER BEHAVIOR AND A/B TESTING

There are many entrepreneurs who shut themselves in their garage and create something for a year or two and then come out again, hoping to explode the market with their product and receive recognition. Sadly, most of these cases end in disappointment, since everything changes very quickly. I've already mentioned the *lean* philosophy, which focuses on creating MVP, making small iterations, and testing them with your early users.

The behavior of users is related to their habits, and changing them is very hard. People always choose the easiest path, so you constantly have to keep thinking about how to remove all obstacles so they can start using your product as simply as possible. Most projects on Kickstarter are *physical*, but they are presented *virtually* through a website, so it's useful to know a bit more about human behavior and their interaction with the website. For that, I'd recommend reading the book *Don't Make Me Think* by Steve Krug about web usability. The name of the book perfectly details the outlook of the user: solve the problem in such a way that I would not have to think—quickly, easily, and simply.

The creator has to be as close to his users as possible to evaluate the situation from their perspective. Using the MVP philosophy, it is always better to make small changes and validate them based on the reactions of the first users. It is okay to hear a user's opinion, but it is more effective to analyze a user's behavior, collect important data, and compare how certain parameters shift after making changes. One of the best examples of this approach is A/B testing, performed by creating newsletters, ads, websites, applications, etc. It helps you evaluate how certain changes affect the user's behavior.

Let's say, you are researching how your website visitors react to the color of a button. After introducing the alteration and doing the A/B testing, you find that the white button is clicked by 23% of the visitors, whereas the black one—by 11%. After testing, you can conclude that a white button on your website brings better results than a black one. If you were simply asking them which they prefer as a question, you would probably get different results, as users would then consider which color they like more—this is exactly the difference between a user's mind and their real behavior.

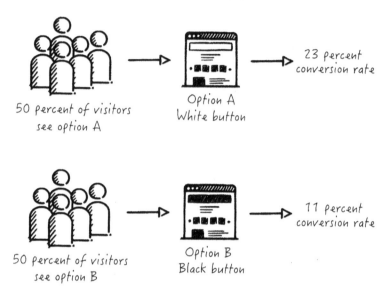

Fig. 14. Example of A/B testing using two website versions with different colored buttons

BUILDING A TEAM

Everyone has strengths and weaknesses and it is worth admitting that we are not talented in all areas. You can easily accomplish small projects alone, but when it comes to bigger goals, you will need the help of other people.

Usually, a team comes to life when a group of like-minded people, who want to achieve the same goal, band together. In this case, each member becomes a partner of the project or company. While interviewing project creators, I've noticed that those who raised higher funds on Kickstarter had at least one colleague in their team. If you are working by yourself, there's a certain level of project complexity that you can manage better with the help of volunteers, assistants, freelancers, or agencies.

Ernestas Klevas, creator of the tea-based social enterprise Tealure, had three people who assisted him: a graphic designer, copywriter and video editor. Ernestas told that volunteering is very popular in Denmark and you can easily find the needed experts by simply adding advertisements in local volunteering portals. People volunteer because they want to gain more experience in their field and add something new to their portfolio. It's great for the project creator as they can easily find people from different fields and get assistance free of charge. However, most volunteers are usually beginners in their area, and this is their part-time activity, so you shouldn't expect very high quality or high work efficiency from them. Moreover, volunteering is only suitable if your project has a social cause.

My book project was commercial, so I didn't even consider asking volunteers for help. Despite this, I accidentally found a professional who worked as a creative director in a big company, who agreed to draw illustrations for my book free of charge. Frankly speaking, I didn't even expect this, but the man was very excited about the work I do and proposed to assist me. As a thank you, I added a credit for him in the book and sent a printed copy once it was published. I also needed experts from other fields, so I hired freelancers to film and edit my project video, proofread and edit the manuscript, design a book cover, create the interior of inner pages, convert the book file to a format suitable for Amazon, etc.

Another option is to work with an agency. There are many types of agencies that specialize in different fields. Both Kickstarter and Indiegogo have a list of agencies and individuals that are considered experts in their field. Later in this book, I'll share one story that belongs to Augustas Alesiunas, co-founder of Food Sniffer. He first hired one of the leading PR agencies from London, but it didn't bring any results, so Food Sniffer then switched to a niche PR agency from Florida that specialized in crowdfunding. This decision changed everything and since then, Food Sniffer has appeared in several popular TV shows and huge online media outlets.

If you have some simple, repetitive work that cannot be automated and requires a human, you can consider hiring virtual assistants who can effectively complete standard jobs for a relatively low rate. To learn more about this, I'd recommend reading the book *The 4-Hour Workweek* by Tim Ferriss.

If there's a more complex job that requires specific knowledge or skills (website development, programming, design, copywriting, translation, etc.), you can hire professional freelancers. I personally use Fiverr, but you can also use other platforms, such as Upwork, Guru,

PeoplePerHour or Freelancer. If you do not know which criteria to select freelancers or agencies by, always ask for recommendations. Most project creators are happy to share their experience.

PRE-LAUNCH

Preparation for a Kickstarter launch usually takes a few months, but there are cases when it lasts a year or more. It all depends on the stage of the idea, the project itself, the funding goal, and the resources available. The result that you achieve during pre-launch has a direct impact on the success of your crowdfunding campaign. Most projects fail because the creator didn't prepare at all or their pre-launch wasn't done well enough. This chapter is the most important, so read it carefully.

The key objective of the pre-launch is to gather a group of potential backers who will eventually become your early backers once the project is launched. That is necessary, because the first days of the campaign are the most important. If you get a significant number of backers during the first day, this will trigger Kickstarter's inner algorithms and your project will appear higher in the platform's search, thus giving you a greater chance to get additional traffic from the Kickstarter users who are browsing campaigns. Kickstarter statistics show that 78% of projects that gathered 20% of their target sum in the first two days were successful projects.

SET YOUR GOAL

The first step is to set a goal. A goal on crowdfunding platforms is set by two criteria: money and time. You have to specify how much money you need to raise for the project to come to life and how long the campaign will take.

When evaluating the project funding goal, you must know all the costs involved. Often the production of a prototype is quite expensive, and in order to reduce the cost of the product, mass production is required. But most mass production companies undertake such projects only when there is a certain number of orders. So if your product needs to be mass produced, you must accurately figure out all the costs: design, layouts, parts, assembly, packaging, shipping, etc. You must also evaluate how long all these tasks will take and when your backers can expect the finished product.

Gediminas, creator of Rubbee, an electric drive for bicycles, said that those who consider mass production for their products should have a well-tested prototype and a complete picture of the manufacturing plan with a cost for each phase. When he launched his first project on Kickstarter, he didn't have a working prototype, so he couldn't precisely estimate the development costs. He was lucky that after his crowdfunding campaign, he received additional funding from investors, because in order to develop the final version of Rubbee and to produce the first batch and ship it to the backers, he spent twice the amount he'd raised during the Kickstarter campaign... And his problems didn't end there. Gediminas thought that he would ship Rubbee by regular post and applied around a $60 shipping fee. However, it turned out that according to the airline regulations, Rubbee was assigned to dangerous cargo and thus shipping costs increased six times, and the creators of Rubbee had to pay that from their pocket. So, learn from others' mistakes and calculate your budget as precisely as possible.

When calculating the minimum project estimate, please note that the cost of logistics is also included in the funding goal, so add this to your budget. You will also have to pay the 5% Kickstarter platform fee and 3–5% for processing credit cards. Moreover, as I have already mentioned, you may lose a few percent due to canceled payments and dropped pledges. Finally, after receiving the money, you will have to pay taxes. So consult a tax administrator in advance to find out what fees you will have to pay, from what amount, and when.

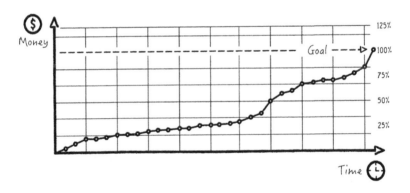

Fig. 15. A goal on crowdfunding platforms is defined by two criteria: money and time

For my goal, I needed an editor, layout designer, illustrator, cover designer, and a printing house. After comparing a few offers, I made a preliminary estimate for the amount of money I would need to self-publish my book. Due to the Kickstarter's *all-or-nothing* principle, I decided to set a lower financial target than I have calculated, as I didn't want to risk not reaching the goal.

It is always better to set a smaller financial goal, because you can achieve it faster and people who regularly review crowdfunding projects pay more attention to those campaigns that have already passed the 100% funding mark. Early success shows that other people trust you, so this adds more credibility for your project, thus encouraging others to pledge for your campaign with more confidence.

Besides, platforms allow you to raise more money than you have initially set. In such cases project authors who have reached their primary target try to encourage their community to strive for a bigger financial goal. Even a specific term—*stretch goals*—has been created, which means that if a certain amount is raised, the author will add some value to their products (for example, they will offer different color models, install additional features, or otherwise improve the primary product version)

Don't pull the financial goal out of thin air. Carefully evaluate all costs, share your budget with other people who have experience in this field, and ask their opinion. If you create something simple, that is not so important, but for complex projects it's a must. Always specify the minimal financial goal. By doing this, you will achieve that goal faster and then you will be able to gather bigger financial support. The Kickstarter platform, your backers, the press... everyone likes a project that has reached its goal swiftly. You can then highlight this achievement in a press release and in updates for your backers, increased six times, and the creators of Rubbee had to pay that from their pocket. So, learn from others' mistakes and calculate your budget as precisely as possible.

When calculating the minimum project estimate, please note that the cost of logistics is also included in the funding goal, so add this to your budget. You will also have to pay the 5% Kickstarter platform fee and 3–5% for processing credit cards. Moreover, as I have already mentioned, you may lose a few percent due to canceled payments and dropped pledges. Finally, after receiving the money, you will have to pay taxes. So consult a tax administrator in advance to find out what fees you will have to pay, from what amount, and when.

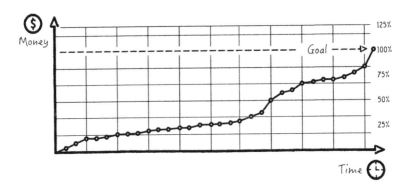

Fig. 15. A goal on crowdfunding platforms is defined by two criteria: money and time

For my goal, I needed an editor, layout designer, illustrator, cover designer, and a printing house. After comparing a few offers, I made a preliminary estimate for the amount of money I would need to self-publish my book. Due to the Kickstarter's *all-or-nothing* principle, I decided to set a lower financial target than I have calculated, as I didn't want to risk not reaching the goal.

It is always better to set a smaller financial goal, because you can achieve it faster and people who regularly review crowdfunding projects pay more attention to those campaigns that have already passed the 100% funding mark. Early success shows that other people trust you, so this adds more credibility for your project, thus encouraging others to pledge for your campaign with more confidence.

Besides, platforms allow you to raise more money than you have initially set. In such cases project authors who have reached their primary target try to encourage their community to strive for a bigger financial goal. Even a specific term—*stretch goals*—has been created, which means that if a certain amount is raised, the author will add some value to their products (for example, they will offer different color models, install additional features, or otherwise improve the primary product version)

Don't pull the financial goal out of thin air. Carefully evaluate all costs, share your budget with other people who have experience in this field, and ask their opinion. If you create something simple, that is not so important, but for complex projects it's a must. Always specify the minimal financial goal. By doing this, you will achieve that goal faster and then you will be able to gather bigger financial support. The Kickstarter platform, your backers, the press... everyone likes a project that has reached its goal swiftly. You can then highlight this achievement in a press release and in updates for your backers, showing that your project has exceeded all expectations.

When choosing the product's delivery date, give yourself more time, rather than less. If you rush to complete the order, you will experience stress and that may cause the product's quality to decrease. Authors of one of the most famous Kickstarter projects, the Coolest Cooler, which raised $13 million, were unable to fulfill their obligations to their backers after two years. As a reason for this delay, they indicated inaccurate manufacturing cost estimates. Why not set lower expectations, then? If you inform your backers that they will get their product in a year, but you manage to complete everything in half a year, you will exceed their initial expectations and they will feel grateful.

Finally, when selecting the project's duration, I recommend setting a 30–35 days period. If the project is too short, you may not get to make the most of all your funding opportunities, and if it is too prolonged, potential backers will get bored and it will be harder for you to retain excitement throughout a lengthy campaign.

ANALYZE SIMILAR CAMPAIGNS

When you have set a clear goal, the next step is to analyze similar campaigns on the crowdfunding platforms. You can search for projects by keyword and sort them by the desired criteria (popularity, date, amount raised, number of backers, etc.). If you don't find similar projects, you can instead research campaigns that simply fall into the same category as yours.

There are a few reasons why analyzing projects is important. First of all, you will see how creators present their project in the video clip, how they try to differentiate from others, what campaign descriptions consist of, and what rewards could be offered. You will also learn if the project was actively shared in social media, and which blogs or news portals have mentioned this project. But most important is that you can contact the project creator directly and ask relevant questions.

I recommend getting in touch with both successful and unsuccessful campaign authors, so that you can gain experience from successful campaigns, and learn from mistakes that caused failure. I've spoken with many creators who managed to bring their ideas to life—most of them were friendly and happily shared their experience with me. This helped me flesh out my project and envisage my campaign strategy.

Kickstarter Project Page

You can find a lot of useful information on the project's page on the Kickstarter platform. By selecting a project on the Kickstarter website and clicking the "Community" tab, you will see which countries and cities backers come from, and how many new and returning backers there are. This information will be especially important if you decide to run ads to drive traffic to your campaign.

Where Backers Come From
Top Countries

United States	30,040 backers
United Kingdom	6,364 backers
Germany	4,497 backers
Canada	4,252 backers
Australia	3,656 backers
Singapore	2,104 backers
Japan	1,833 backers
Netherlands	1,809 backers
France	1,615 backers
Spain	1,423 backers

Fig. 16. The "Community" section of the Kickstarter platform

Next, click on the "Embed" icon and copy the link under the "Project short link" note. At the end of the link, add a "+" symbol and enter it into your browser. You will be redirected to Bitly (https://bitly.com), which allows you to shorten links and shows where the visitors came from by percentage.

If you are not registered on Bitly, you will only see the number of clicks on specific dates. You may sign up for a free account and then you will also see the statistics of referring websites (referrers) and locations (countries). More detailed statistics are available only with paid accounts. It's worth mentioning that Bitly tracks only shortened links and it usually represents just a small portion of a campaign's traffic, so the data you see may not correlate with the real numbers. But overall, Bitly is very useful when you launch your own project as it allows you to track your marketing campaigns and compare their performance.

There's also some interesting information that you may find by clicking on the creator's profile. As I mentioned previously, smaller campaigns are run by one person, but those that achieve higher funding goals usually have some collaborators. In Fig. 17 you can see a list of collaborators that participated in the POWERUP paper airplane project on Kickstarter. You can then contact the project creator and ask his opinion about specific agencies that they have hired to do marketing for their campaign.

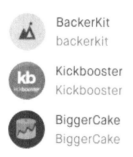

Fig. 17. Collaborators on the POWERUP paper airplane project

Finally, check the "Comments" section on the campaign page. It gives an idea about what's relevant for potential backers, what doubts they have, and how creators communicate with them.

Kicktraq

Kicktraq is like Google Analytics, but made for the Kickstarter platform. This tool allows you to see the state of the project, the number of backers, the amount raised, a financing graph, project updates, and other useful information.

I recommend using the "Daily Data" graph that shows pledges, backers, and comments per day. When you open the graph, which depicts the amount raised each day, pay attention to the days that raised the most. You may notice that many projects received the highest funding on their first day. This means that the project author did a good pre-launch and gathered a group of potential backers before launching the project. Sometimes, there's also an increase over the last two days because backers are reminded that the campaign is ending soon, and the feeling of urgency encourages them to support the project.

However, there may be a peak in funding on a random day. You should find out what events corresponded with an increase in pledges. You may enter the project title in Google to check if there were some news stories or blog posts published on that specific date. But Google doesn't index everything, so you can also review campaign updates and social network profiles of the project you research, because the creators usually share more significant events publicly. Also, don't hesitate to contact the project author and ask directly what events led to pledge increases on specific days.

BiggerCake

BiggerCake is another tool that allows you to analyze revenue, backers, rewards, popularity, community, and all-time ranking. It gives even more data than Kicktraq and information is displayed in a more user-friendly way. However, BiggerCake appeared in 2018, so you cannot use it to analyze older projects.

Advanced Campaign Analysis

No tool will help you get as much information as you can gather yourself. If you want to get the real picture, it is recommended you analyze 5–10 similar projects. To illustrate what analysis of the project consists of, I will give you the example of PARKIS, a bicycle parking system project.

When you open the "PARKIS—space saving bicycle lift" project (see Fig. 18), you will find that it was created by Giedre. If you click on her profile, you will see that she has created three projects. By opening the first project, we can see that the product is the same (PARKIS), but the first funding in 2015 was unsuccessful. The second attempt was successful, so we can assume that the project authors did something different this time, because not only did they raise the required funding, but also exceeded it greatly. We will analyze this project in more detail.

PARKIS – space saving bicycle lift

Fig. 18. The PARKIS project page on the Kickstarter platform

As I already mentioned, it is always worth writing to the project author and asking what caused their project's success and how they attracted their backers. By doing this, you will save a lot of time and will get information which you cannot find when using previously mentioned tools, search engines, or other methods. If the author does not respond, you can still do project analysis independently.

Right-click on the PARKIS main project photo and select "Search Google for image." It helps to quickly discover visually similar images from around the web. In the search results, you will see various websites which mention PARKIS. Pay attention to the dates when these posts were published. You can easily find in the campaign's page or on Kicktraq that the PARKIS project was started on November 10, 2016 and finished on December 10, 2016. This means that if a news article or a blog post was published during the campaign, it could have resulted in additional traffic, but if the post was published after the project ended, it could not have had any influence on funding.

After making this presumption, we can see that information about PARKIS on the outsideonline.com, thegadgetflow.com, trendhunter.com, and dudeiwantthat.com portals was published only after the project finished. It means that these portals did not have any influence on the funding of PARKIS campaign. Of the blogs found, more traffic could have been the cause of only two: gigadgets.com and bridde.com, because they both published their article during the project.

So far, we have only conducted a search of one image. To get a better picture, we will extend the search by writing "parkis bicycle lift" into the Google search box. I've looked through the first three Google pages, and was able to find nine blogs (including the ones found previously) that posted an article about PARKIS during the project. We can conclude that searching the web is more effective than searching by image.

Let's compare these blogs and news portals by using Similarweb (https://www.similarweb.com). Here is the list of portals that published articles about PARKIS and their global position (in parentheses) by the total website traffic:

- **digitaltrends.com** (1,443) is the 20th portal in its category (News and Media > Technology News)—a fairly high position. The readers commented on the article and it was shared 59 times on Facebook.
- **metro.co.uk** (1,608) is a general news portal

that only shared the PARKIS video, but did not provide more information.

- **newatlas.com** (7,358), previously known as Gizmag, is a well-known portal for newly developed technologies, so the PARKIS project could have been relevant for readers.

- **unofficialnetworks.com** (83,875) this portal is mostly oriented towards winter sports, so it was not well suited for the theme of PARKIS.

- **gigadgets.com** (178,633) has more than 7 million followers on their Facebook profile, which is definitely an impressive number. It is also noteworthy that the slogan of the GiGadgets website ("The latest, coolest, and smartest technology and gadgets available") matches the innovative PARKIS idea. Moreover, the article has visitor comments that ask where they can purchase the product. So the impact of this website is definitely positive.

- **sharpmagazine.com** (401,134) is a men's lifestyle magazine. I am not sure if this could be a potential PARKIS audience.

- **eta.co.uk** (489,593) is a transport (including bicycles) and travel insurance portal. Their article did not have any comments and was not shared, so I don't think it had any impact on funding.

- **bridde.com** (745,763) is quite a new project, which does not have its audience yet. Its Facebook profile was created on 2016 October and has only received 78 likes. After sharing this PARKIS article on their Facebook profile, they were not able to engage with their followers.

- **startingthingsup.com** (2,583,424) is a very

low-ranking portal. The article here was viewed 863 times, which is too low a number to have any impact.

It is fairly clear that the PARKIS project has attracted considerable attention from news portals and blogs. But knowing the list of portals that wrote about PARKIS doesn't tell us where the most backers came from. By using the aforementioned Kicktraq, we can analyze the project's daily financing graph (see Fig. 19).

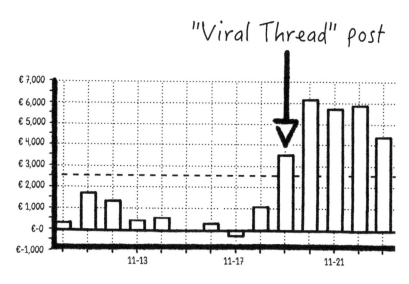

Fig. 19. Financing graph of the PARKIS project

As you see, there's no peak in funding during the first days, which means that the project creators did not prepare well and did not have a sufficient list of potential backers prior to launching the campaign. On November 17, someone even canceled their pledge. But what exactly happened during November 18–19, when the campaign results suddenly shot up?

If we were to look at the posts of the PARKIS Facebook profile (see Fig. 20), we would notice something unusual. It turns out that on November 18, 2016, the news agency Viral Thread, which has almost 14 million followers on their Facebook profile, shared their own customized version of the PARKIS video. As a result, it was viewed over 3 million times!

Fig. 20. A PARKIS post on Facebook

The result was truly impressive! This viral video was the main factor that led to the PARKIS campaign success on the Kickstarter platform. But reviewing each post of a particular project in social media is time-consuming, so it is always worth remembering an alternative—you can always contact the author of the project. That is exactly what I did. After talking to the author of the PARKIS project, I found out much more than I possibly could have any other way.

Getting in Touch with the Project Author

While I was in touch with people who wanted to introduce their idea on Kickstarter, I noticed that they were all slightly afraid of approaching other project authors. I heard excuses such as "They are our competitors," "Why should they share their experience if we might take their clients," etc. These types of thoughts are mostly provoked due to lack of self-confidence or distrust in other people. But consider this: what is the worst-case scenario of trying to make contact? For various reasons, the author might not respond or refuse to give you the information. But on the other hand, you might get great tips, learn from other person's mistakes, and understand what the most valuable actions are that can make your project successful.

Once I was researching similar projects for the company DigiFrame. It was a smart e-ink display that showed the most relevant information to the user, such as weather, calendar, to do list, etc. There were similar products in the market, but only a few of them had raised money through crowdfunding. Probably the most similar project was a digital epaper sticky note called SeeNote (almost identical to DigiFrame in its appearance and functionality). I started searching the web for information on this project and found out that the author of this project had decided to make pre-orders directly through his website instead of choosing a crowdfunding platform.

There were a lot of articles on highly authoritative portals that were responding to SeeNote positively. But the product did not have its own website, which was strange. After some time, I found an article by the author of the SeeNote project, in which he announced that the product would no longer be developed, and the money would be returned to the backers. I decided to contact the author and find out what methods he'd used to raise money and why the project had been canceled in the end. Here's the email I wrote to him.

> Hi Matt,
>
> I've been reading a lot about your project Seenote and it's a pity that you've decided to no longer develop it. It seemed like a great project with nice publicity!
>
> The reason I'm contacting you is that we're planning to launch a similar project, a smart e-ink display DigiFrame (you can find more info in our web and Facebook page). We're in the process of product development and hope to launch our Kickstarter in October.
>
> You've gone through this journey yourself, so I'd really appreciate if you could share your experience, what has worked, and what didn't (especially the reason why you decided to stop development).
>
> Could we discuss this by Skype call/chat?
>
> P.S. If you're not available, we can continue by email.
>
> Thanks,
>
> Vilius

I got an answer after a few hours.

> Hey Vilius, Thanks for reaching out. I would be happy to discuss this with you.
>
> Here are some times that work for me below.
>
> When looks good for you?

We agreed the date for a Skype chat and during our

conversation, I learned a lot of important things. The SeeNote project had raised $200,000 from pre-orders through its own landing page in two and a half months. I got all the information on how this happened, what worked, and what didn't. During the interview, I wrote down three A4-sized pages of notes that contained:

- the number of contacts (email addresses) gathered,
- the statistics of emails opens and clicks,
- the number of followers on social media,
- tactics for communicating with potential clients,
- the number of site visitors who submitted orders,
- the ways that press attention was obtained,
- three main factors that helped raise the required sum.

It was hard to believe that a person could devote so much time and share such important information with a stranger. Most people would probably keep this information confidential and would only share it with the closest people. But there are always people who sincerely try to help others attempting to achieve similar goals. Undoubtedly, Matthew Bleistern, author of the SeeNote project, is one of these people, because not only did he benevolently share his experience and the most important details, but he also gave advice that was especially helpful in preparing the project. And that is not all! At the end of the conversation, he mentioned one influential person working in this market, and offered to introduce me. So, I was really fortunate to have written to

Matthew.

Summarizing this story, one can make a simple conclusion: it is always worth getting in touch with authors of similar projects. If they do not reply, or refuse to help, then no worries. But if you manage to make a contact, you may receive valuable information that will help you bring your idea to life. It is always better to consult with a person who has already achieved something that you are trying to achieve now.

TARGET AUDIENCE

At the beginning of the chapter, I mentioned that the main goal of pre-launch is to gather a sufficient number of *potential* backers (in this book I will also use the synonym *lead* to define a potential client) before introducing the project. I'm emphasizing the word *potential* because it defines how many people from the contacts that you've gathered will eventually become your backers. The more *potential* they are, the better *conversion rate* you can expect.

Target audience is a group of people defined by certain criteria, such as age, gender, interests, location, income, education, etc., who are facing problems that your product solves. Those people are your potential customers. Knowing your target audience is a must for every business. The more information you have, the easier it will be to find the segment that will be most interested in your project. It is much more effective to inform people that find your project relevant than to shove your product in everyone's faces. If you know the problems and needs of your target clients, you will be able to prepare a message that will affect them emotionally and will also interest them in your project. If someone is saying that their target audience is people from all over the world, from age 18 to 55, it means that this person doesn't have any clue about their clients.

One mistake that a lot of start-ups, entrepreneurs and creators make when they conduct market research or target market data is to simply ask those close to them. This is a massive *no*. Your friends and family are compelled not to criticize you. You will learn nothing from their feedback because they will most likely tell you what you want to hear, and it offers no benefit to you. You need to go to your actual target market. Also, be careful with your wording, don't just hand them a product and say, "would this solve your problem?" You need to find out if they have a problem first, afterwards, have them discuss a solution with you and you can add your own ideas. Show them your product (or a prototype) and get their opinion towards the end.

If you're creating something for the first time, it will be harder for you to determine who your potential clients are, but you shouldn't worry about this much. I'll share a few examples of how to gather a crowd of people who will support your project and will share experience of other creators so that you can learn from them and adapt their methods for your case.

GATHER YOUR CROWD (FREE METHODS)

There's a reason why we discussed *what target audience is and what it isn't* in the previous section. You must understand the difference between your target audience (people who will buy and use your product) and people who know who you are and who will support you, even if what you create is completely irrelevant for them.

If you want to launch a campaign with a minimal or no budget and your goal is to raise a few thousand dollars, support from people you know will be very important. I know this because I launched my campaign with no marketing budget and all pledges came from people who already knew me—my personal network, business relationships and other acquaintances that I made throughout my life. In this section, I will share what methods you can use to gather your crowd. Those methods are free and require just your personal time.

On the other hand, if you want to raise tens or hundreds of thousand dollars, or if you don't want to waste your time experimenting with free methods to gather your crowd, you may skip this section and focus only on generating leads that match your target audience. In this case, you should be ready to spend around 30% of what you plan to raise on marketing. We will talk about this later in this book.

Personal Relationships

If you are creating something new, the first people to find

out will most likely be your relatives, friends, and acquaintances. These people know and trust you, and most of them will definitely support your idea. Even if the product you are creating is completely irrelevant to them, their support is still important, because Kickstarter's algorithm takes into account the number of new backers (even if they pledge just $1).

Most probably, you have some preferred communication channel that you use with your contacts. It can be a simple phone call, some messaging platform (WhatsApp, Viber, Facebook Messenger, etc.), social network, or email. I recommend dividing your personal contacts into a few groups, depending on the way you use to communicate with them. Prepare a personalized text and then outreach to your contacts.

Make sure you specify what you are planning to do and what you want from them. You can mention that if the project is relevant for them, they will be able make a pledge and choose your product as a reward. If the project is irrelevant, but they still want to support you, they can make a symbolic $1 pledge without any reward. Explain to them the importance of this action. If the Kickstarter platform detects a rapid growth of backers, your project may appear higher up in the search results, which will provide additional backers from the platform. As it is a pre-launch stage, at the end of your message or email, it's enough to ask if they would like to be notified when the campaign is launched. That's all. When you get their permission, you can add them to the appropriate list.

I knew that my book about VoIP business was quite

specific and would be irrelevant to all of my friends. So I had to overcome myself to ask them to support my project. Pitching friends and asking for their support was really hard for me. Even though I had a few hundred friends on Facebook, I did not contact them all. I picked about 50 friends and sent them private messages. After explaining what I was doing, I asked if they would like to be notified when the Kickstarter campaign would start. If they said "Yes," I asked them to provide their email address. Looking at it retrospectively, this wasn't necessary, as I could have easily sent private messages through Facebook without spending too much time. But back then, I thought that by asking for an email I'd be able to communicate the launch more effectively.

I understood that my book wasn't relevant to my friends, so I didn't expect any of them to back my project. But to my surprise, more than half of them supported my project and not just with a symbolic amount. Some of them bought the book and one or two donated a few hundred dollars.

Recalling how difficult it was to ask for help and what kind of gratitude I felt for my friends and acquaintances who supported this project, I can safely say that all of this was worth doing. When asking for help and providing it, we make our friendship bonds stronger. If you are surrounding yourself with the right type of people, they will be always happy to help.

Business Relationships

This list includes all people with whom you share a

common activity. They can be your potential and existing clients, partners, or people you have met at conferences or seminars. It is ideal when a concept that you want to bring to life on the Kickstarter platform is related to the area in which you have been working for a while. Because of this, you will have accumulated a number of business contacts, which will really be useful in this case. Unlucky are those who do not gather or systemize their contacts. But nowadays, it is hard to find an entrepreneur who does not use a customer relationship management (CRM) system or the business contact social network LinkedIn.

As I suggested doing with personal contacts, the same rule applies here. Choose those channels that you use for regular communication. You can send private messages via LinkedIn or you can export all contacts into a CSV file and then use this list to send personalized emails. If you use Gmail, I recommend trying Yesware or Yet Another Email Merge, which is a Gmail extension that allows you to send personalized emails to a group of people. Such emails will look exactly the same as if you sent them regularly.

However, you can use email merge programs only if you have a relatively small mailing list. E.g. Yet Another Email Merge allows you to send up to 400 emails within 24 hours. But if you use the maximum possible limit, you risk being captured by spam filters and as a result, your email may end up in the spam box. To make sure that your email reaches the inbox of your contact, I would recommend choosing around 150 emails per email blast within 24 hours as a safe limit. If you have a bigger list, use email merge programs only for the most important contacts, and to notify others, use newsletter programs that are meant to handle huge lists (we will talk about them more later in this chapter). Also, remember to ask for permission to send emails and include possibility to unsubscribe from your emails.

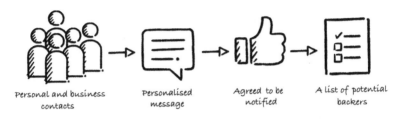

Fig. 21. How to turn personal and business contacts into potential backers

Every Acquaintance Can Be Useful

When you meet a person, you never know in which direction the acquaintanceship may go. I will tell you the story of how one acquaintance surpassed all my expectations.

Five years ago, the company director and I were discussing how to improve our company's sales results. We had both read the book *Predictable Revenue: Turn Your Business into a Sales Machine with the $100 Million Best Practices of Salesforce.com* by Aaron Ross and Marylou Tyler. This book described a predictable sales process, which we thought could be adapted to our case. We thought: "Who could we consult on how to implement this process better than the authors of the book?" So, we decided to give it a shot and contact the authors of this book, without knowing what to expect.

We were worried that they would respond at all and if they did, whether we could afford their consultation fees. To our surprise, Marylou Tyler, the co-author of the book, not only responded, but offered to arrange a call and discuss our case and how she could help. The conversation shocked us even more. She said: "I only work with clients from the USA and have not yet tried remote consultations, but if you agree to be my guinea pigs, we can try working together." I almost fell out of my chair: the bestseller author had just agreed to consult us for free!

We consulted with Marylou each week and tried to implement the sales process for half a year, but we were unable to create a process that would pay us back and improve our sales, so we had to give up on the idea. Nevertheless, I was grateful and kept in touch with Marylou and emailed her once in a while. After a year, before introducing my book campaign on the Kickstarter platform, I decided to write her and tell her about my old dream to publish a book. She responded and told me she was happy that I was progressing, and asked me to inform her when the campaign started.

After introducing the project, I informed her once more, but to be blunt, I did not expect anything, since the book was not in her area. But something unbelievable happened. On Friday evening, I checked the funding progress of my campaign and I was left completely shocked: Marylou had supported my project with $800! At first, I was confused and thought: "Why would such an influential person support my personal project?" But after some time, and reading one of her articles, everything made sense. This is what she wrote in one of her LinkedIn posts:

> I feel it is my responsibility to share the expertise I implement for companies to those who request my assistance.
>
> To facilitate this effort, I mentor 2–3 sales professionals on a pro-bono basis each quarter. My students reach out to me directly (since I teach this style of sales process, I applaud their efforts).
>
> I ask little in return:
>
> Take this mentorship as seriously as I do.
>
> Be on time for our calls.
>
> Do the homework I've given you.
>
> Execute the process I'm teaching you.
>
> Here is the sad statistic I want to share with you today. Of the 32 sales professionals I've mentored over the past 4 years, only 3 completed our sessions (9.4%).
>
> 29 (90.6%) ...
>
> Canceled phone sessions with me minutes before our scheduled call
>
> Did not complete the homework I assigned
>
> Lost focus (stuck in urgent-but-not-important activities at work)
>
> Just plain gave up
>
> And the 3 who finished?
>
> All 3 achieved and even outperformed the goals we originally

set together:

One has written a book.

One is now a Chief Revenue Officer.

Another has gone on to become a speaker and noted authority in his field.

All have used the outreach engine to further their sales efforts.

Which one of this group are you, truly?

What lessons can you learn from this story?

- **Compliment a person if you genuinely value what they do or if their work changed something in your life for the better.** I expect that you read a lot of interesting articles, books, listen to podcasts, participate in various conferences, seminars, or other events. If you find some content valuable, tell this to an author or speaker directly or by email. Trust me, they will be happy to know that someone is genuinely interested and appreciates their work.

- **Start making acquaintances as early as possible.** After reading a book you liked or visiting an interesting blog, instantly write to the author. When listening to a great seminar, ask the speaker a question or chat to them after the seminar. Act quickly because the more you think about how to approach a person, the bigger probability that you will never do this.

- **Think about the addressee and not about yourself.** When attempting to start a relationship with someone, don't ask for a favor instantly. If you do so, you will most likely be ignored, and your relationship will not move any further. Influential people get tons of messages with different requests, and they make a very fast decision about whom to respond to. So instead of asking for a favor, think about how you can create value for them. Commend them for the great insights in the article; tell the story of how their book changed your life.

- **Do not create excessive expectations when you start a relationship.** Do not get in touch with anyone only hoping for them to immediately support your project. Your intentions will be easily noticed when communicating. Start new relationships because a particular person is interesting to you, without expecting that they will help you in the future. First create value for them and leave everything else to the natural flow. If it happens that they return your favor, let this be a pleasant surprise rather than an expectation.

Followers

Before getting into this topic, I will clarify the meaning of a follower in this book. A follower is a stranger to you who has subscribed to your newsletter or follows you or your project on social networks. Your friend or business partner may also follow you, but we have already discussed that group of people, so now, we will talk about followers who you do not know and who do not belong to a personal or business group.

You probably associate followers with an audience of hundreds of thousands of people that celebrities gather. But nowadays, even a regular person who uploads selfies on Instagram can have followers. Your project can also have followers, if you are creating something interesting and you are ready to constantly share relevant content to your target audience on social networks.

You should begin by creating profiles on the channels that your target audience uses the most (Facebook, Instagram, Twitter, YouTube, LinkedIn, etc.). After creating a profile, you have to constantly upload new and interesting content (articles, videos, photos, infographics, etc.) that would interest your followers and provoke them to engage with the information you share. To find and periodically post interesting content on different platforms is not easy, so you can use social media management tools, such as Hootsuite or Buffer. They allow you to upload content in one place and distribute it at certain times to the platforms you have picked. Do not forget that the posts should be different, depending on what site you are posting them on. But if you think that creating different posts will take too much time, just pick one social network and be active on that.

By constantly creating relevant content, your community will be more immersed, and your project will gain popularity. It is even more important to constantly grow your community. Achieving this organically is not easy, especially when social networks such as Facebook change their algorithms to reduce organic growth and companies or projects must buy ads in order to reach their audience and attract new followers.

It is also important to have your followers' email addresses, so that additionally you can communicate with them via emails. The probability that your followers will notice your email is a few times higher than the probability that they will see your post in a social network. That's why it's so important to collect emails. To request an email, you can use internal forms in social networks or point your followers to your landing page, where they can leave their contact details.

You can make the most from your followers when you share information on a certain niche, before you even consider starting a crowdfunding campaign. A great example on how to use your followers to support your project is the beauty and fashion blog advanced. style, which is devoted "to capturing the sartorial savvy of the senior set." Ari Seth Cohen, the creator of the Advanced Style blog, together with his friend Lina Plioplyte, decided to crowdfund the film of the same title: *Advanced Style*. Since Ari's blog had a decent number of followers, it helped the creators to not only reach their primary financial goal on the Kickstarter platform, but to also surpass it. Later, Ari Seth Cohen also published the *Advanced Style* book, which achieved great success on Amazon.

So, if you have any sort of hobby, are interested in a specific niche, and want to share information that could be relevant to a specific audience, start working on it as early as possible. If you create useful content on a regular basis that thousands of people start to like, you will establish a group of followers that is worth a lot these days. Once you achieve a significant number of engaged followers, you'll be able to crowdfund a project related to your niche much easier.

Direct Contact with Potential Backers

You can also find potential backers or people that could help you directly. This process takes longer, but you will be able to easily compare the progress and results after evaluating other methods. If you see that the results of using this method are acceptable, you can describe the process and assign the job to virtual assistants who can do this at a relatively low hourly rate.

I tried to run an experiment and apply this strategy for the virtual training assistant Ovao, whose target audience was swimmers and swimming coaches. After simply entering "swimming coach email" into Google, I found many USA-based universities and colleges that provide contact information for their swimming coaches in their website. The structure was more or less the same on all websites, so I managed to gather approximately 130 contact details of swimming coaches and systemized the data (see Table 2) within two hours. To make it more efficient you can use data scraping tools that will capture contact details directly from the website.

Name	Title	Email
Megan	Assistant Coach	
Trevor	Head Coach	
Fernando	Senior Assistant Coach	
Doug	Assistant Coach	
Matt	Head Coach	

Kit	Assistant Coach	
Jim	Head Men's Swimming Coach	
Caroline	Women's Swimming Coach	
Blake	Men's Swimming and Diving Coach	
Stephen	Assistant Coach	
Janko	Director of Swimming and Head Coach	
Ingrid	Lead Coach	
Geoff	Lead Coach	
Callum	Assistant Coach	

Table 2. A sample list of swimming coaches in USA

I used the previously mentioned tool Yet Another Email Merge to send personalized emails. As you can see, you may insert custom fields from the list, such as first name, title, and website. In my case, I used just the *name* and the *website* fields (from where I found their contact details) to personalize emails.

The email that I sent looked like this:

Hi {Name},

My name is Vilius and I found your contact in the {website}.

We're developing a virtual swimming coach that helps to improve swimming performance by displaying different parameters (such as heart rate) in real time. Currently it's in the prototype stage and we're trying to collect professional feedback from swimming coaches like you to make Ovao better.

So I'm contacting you with a simple question.

What are the key parameters that you monitor now and how do you do that?

In total, 13% of the swimming coaches responded to the email. Most answers were detailed, containing great tips and useful information. As it was just an experiment, I didn't follow up with a request about whether they would like to be notified once the project was launched. But by evaluating their answers, I presumed that at least half of them would be interested to know when the project was launched.

Search for target audience   Send personalised email   Get permission to be notified   A list of potential backers

Fig. 22. How to turn your target audience to potential backers

This experience is interesting because you can estimate the cost per potential backer. In portals like Upwork, Fiverr, Freelancer, etc., you can find lots of offers to gather contacts. For $10 you can get 100 email addresses of a target audience. In my given example, 13% responded with an interest, so let's assume that 5% of recipients would agree to be notified once the project was launched. This means that if we hire a virtual assistant to gather 100 contacts for $10 and 5% become leads, then each potential backer will cost us $10/(100*0.05) = \$2$. You can compare this price with the cost of advertising on Facebook and evaluate which process allows you to generate leads at a lower price.

Please note that even though a low price per lead is important, it doesn't tell you anything about lead *quality*, which determines how well they will convert to backers. You'll truly know this only once your project is launched. Before that, you can just make some assumptions based on their answers to your email or their messages in social networks.

The Search for Superbackers With Krowdster

Judging by their number of backed projects, some backers can be called *superbackers*. Kickstarter adds a "SuperBacker" badge to the person's profile if they have supported more than 25 projects with pledges of at least $10 in the past year. I believe that the majority of supporters are happy with this recognition and status.

As a target audience, these people are "warmed up" leads, because they already know what Kickstarter is and are acquainted with the possible risks and the processes of backing a campaign. It's not a secret that many project creators think about how to find those superbackers and engage with them. This has piqued my interest and encouraged me to find out more.

One of the solutions is called Krowdster. They claim to offer the world's largest searchable crowdfunding backer directory that contains the data of over 4 million Kickstarter and Indiegogo backers. The directory can be used to search for potential backers by category, the number of supported projects, and geographic location.

Once you apply your filters, you'll be able to see the backer's name, city, country, Kickstarter or Indiegogo profile, the number of supported projects, and their profiles on social networks. You can export this list to a CSV file and use the *lookalike audience* function for advertising on Facebook (you will find out more on this in later chapters). Or you can simply contact them privately via social networks.

I didn't expect much from Krowdster, but I decided to try it simply out of curiosity. The project I worked on was a book, so I was looking for backers on Kickstarter who supported similar projects. I filtered backers by the following criteria: Kickstarter platform, publishing category, and >20 backed projects. There was a total of 40,321 backers found, according to this filter.

I exported this list and we first tried to use this data to create an audience for Facebook ads as Krowdster suggested. But after experimenting with a few ad sets, I noticed that this data had poor quality (at least in our case) because the engagement from this target audience was very low, compared to what we had achieved with other audiences by simply combining interests that we thought were relevant for our project. So I decided to try another method—contacting backers directly.

I didn't want to spend too much time, so I dedicated an hour to go through filtered backers one by one. My goal was to find out how many relevant contacts I'd be able to collect within this time. The first thing I noticed was that the publishing category is actually very wide and includes not only books, but also videos, music, radio, podcasts, etc. As a result, many of the filtered backers were completely irrelevant. When I finally found the first backer that could have suited our project, I noticed that the Facebook profile shown next to him wasn't his personal profile—it was just some project that he had done some time ago... Meaning I had to look for his contact details by another means. As a result, I managed to find two relevant backers in one hour. That was too much time to spend and even outsourcing this task didn't make sense, so I decided not to explore Krowdster possibilities further.

There's one method, though, which I have not tried and which is recommended by the Krowdster platform itself. It allows you to automatically follow the selected backers on Twitter. The website's statistics predict that approximately 10% of people that you start following, become your followers. Then, the system will automatically send a greeting message to these followers, where you will be able to add a link to a site for collecting contacts. That is how, according to Krowdster, you will be able to gather an audience for your Kickstarter campaign. The method seems quite logical, but it is hard to tell to what degree it works. I think the backers in that directory are constantly being "spammed" and receive lots of messages. So in order to get their attention, you have to try hard, as the competition is big.

Whatever impression you've gathered here, don't be in a hurry to buy Krowdster's services. First, just subscribe to the platform's newsletter. I've noticed that they offer constant discounts. A 50% discount does not surprise me anymore, because over four months, I was offered it four times. The best deal I got was 50% OFF which was $44.50 per month for their Backer Directory. The sum is relatively small enough to experiment, so I leave this for you to decide if it's worth a shot.

Using Twitter Hack

This hack was shared by crowdfunding expert Samit Patel, who has reviewed this book and agreed to share his experience. He used this method for a few campaigns and mentioned that it has worked much better than using Krowdster.

The idea of this method is to approach users, who have backed a similar product in Kickstarter. Samit Patel tried this method with Blocks project (the world's first modular smartwatch) which raised over $1.6 million in Kickstarter. They researched other smartwatch campaigns and decided to target Twitter users who posted "I just backed Pebble on Kickstarter." Here's a step by step process:

- Put this into Google search: 'site: twitter.com I just backed xyz Kickstarter' or 'site:twitter.com I just backed xyz on Indiegogo', where xyz is the name of a similar product to yours
- This gives you results of Twitter users who have backed similar projects in Kickstarter or Indiegogo
- Now you can engage with these people through Twitter: follow them, like, retweet and comment on their posts. Don't spam

- When you finally launch, you can tweet them and let them know about you.

Another way to get even more people is to target backer management services like Backerkit. They help with things like making sure backer addresses are correct, doing upsells on products and managing surveys. Backerkit encourages people to share tweets. In this case, put this line into Google search: 'site: twitter.com @backerkit and add your competitor product. As a result, you'll get a list of Twitter users that can potentially be your new backers.

BackerClub

BackerClub is a platform that unifies backers that are active on Kickstarter and Indiegogo. Based on the data from the BackerClub platform, its members have supported almost a million projects, with each member supporting more than a hundred projects on average. This has really intrigued me, and as a project creator, I would love to take advantage of this platform. However, you need to pay a fee of $379 to upload your project to the platform (I am sure that just like in Krowdster's case, you may expect discounts). But it is promising that you will only have to pay if you get the results—i.e. if you collect less than $379 on the BackerClub platform, it will cost you nothing. Sounds good so far.

If you want to encourage the platform's users to back your project, you will have to give them a special reward: 15–25% discount, a free additional item, and a chance to get a higher cost reward for a smaller sum. BackerClub says that a project on average gets a 300% *return on investment (ROI)*, which does sound impressive. However, you can collect $380, which means that the $379 fee will be charged and you will receive only $1 in exchange for a 15–20% discount for each of the rewards a member of the BackerClub chooses. So, the risk remains. The platform also says that before submitting a project, you can receive feedback from members on which parts of the project are to be corrected.

Now let's go back to the other side—the BackerClub members supporting the projects. Why do they back them? Their motives are simple. They get special discounts or exclusive rewards that Kickstarter or Indiegogo backers do not get. In order to objectively evaluate the perspective of a member of the BackerClub, I tried to register and become a member myself.

First of all, I was slightly surprised by the fact that I had to add "Member of the BackerClub" to my Kickstarter profile description. If you do not do this, you are not allowed to register. After editing my biography, I was finally able to register. I had backed three projects back then, and that was enough to become a member. My expectation—that the only people on their system were ones who had backed 20, 50, or more projects—was now gone. I understood that becoming a member was quite easy and every person paying $9.95 per month could become an "elite" member.

When I spoke with Ernest, creator of Tealure, he said that he had paid about $80 for access to the BackerClub platform, but only 4–5 members made pledges—so, after

- When you finally launch, you can tweet them and let them know about you.

Another way to get even more people is to target backer management services like Backerkit. They help with things like making sure backer addresses are correct, doing upsells on products and managing surveys. Backerkit encourages people to share tweets. In this case, put this line into Google search: 'site: twitter.com @backerkit and add your competitor product. As a result, you'll get a list of Twitter users that can potentially be your new backers.

BackerClub

BackerClub is a platform that unifies backers that are active on Kickstarter and Indiegogo. Based on the data from the BackerClub platform, its members have supported almost a million projects, with each member supporting more than a hundred projects on average. This has really intrigued me, and as a project creator, I would love to take advantage of this platform. However, you need to pay a fee of $379 to upload your project to the platform (I am sure that just like in Krowdster's case, you may expect discounts). But it is promising that you will only have to pay if you get the results—i.e. if you collect less than $379 on the BackerClub platform, it will cost you nothing. Sounds good so far.

If you want to encourage the platform's users to back your project, you will have to give them a special reward: 15–25% discount, a free additional item, and a chance to get a higher cost reward for a smaller sum. BackerClub says that a project on average gets a 300% *return on investment* (*ROI*), which does sound impressive. However, you can collect $380, which means that the $379 fee will be charged and you will receive only $1 in exchange for a 15–20% discount for each of the rewards a member of the BackerClub chooses. So, the risk remains. The platform also says that before submitting a project, you can receive feedback from members on which parts of the project are to be corrected.

Now let's go back to the other side—the BackerClub members supporting the projects. Why do they back them? Their motives are simple. They get special discounts or exclusive rewards that Kickstarter or Indiegogo backers do not get. In order to objectively evaluate the perspective of a member of the BackerClub, I tried to register and become a member myself.

First of all, I was slightly surprised by the fact that I had to add "Member of the BackerClub" to my Kickstarter profile description. If you do not do this, you are not allowed to register. After editing my biography, I was finally able to register. I had backed three projects back then, and that was enough to become a member. My expectation—that the only people on their system were ones who had backed 20, 50, or more projects—was now gone. I understood that becoming a member was quite easy and every person paying $9.95 per month could become an "elite" member.

When I spoke with Ernest, creator of Tealure, he said that he had paid about $80 for access to the BackerClub platform, but only 4–5 members made pledges—so, after deducting platform fees, Ernest's project did not receive any financial benefits. Other project creators I've spoken to didn't use BackerClub.

Before deciding whether to use BackerClub or not, talk to a few authors who have used BackerClub's services. Take their reviews into account and decide whether it is worth testing this service out.

Gathering Contacts from Social Media, Forums and Other Target Groups

When you have your target audience figured out, you should analyze what websites or groups they visit. These groups could be on social networks, various forums, discussions, specialized websites, etc. When you have found the right websites and groups, get acquainted with their rules, just so you do not get banned.

After joining relevant groups, try to be active: ask questions, encourage others to express their opinion, leave your comments, etc. Then create a brief and clear post on what you are doing, explaining why the members of the group or forum might be interested. At the end of your post, encourage them to register at your landing page to be the first to know once your project is launched. Some groups don't allow new members to post links—that's why it's a good practice to be more active in a group before sharing a link.

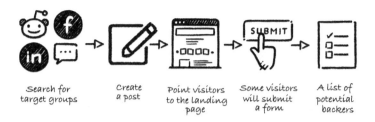

Fig. 23. How to gather potential backers from target groups

By using this strategy, the Pisound team gathered approximately one thousand contacts in just 24 hours! And the best part was that they didn't have to spend anything on advertising! How did they manage it? Everything started from the target audience. The potential Pisound users were people who liked high-quality audio, who knew how to solder, had a Raspberry Pi microcomputer and were interested in DIY ideas. These people are very active, enthusiastic, and are happy to share relevant information in target groups.

First, the Pisound team found a few groups that their target audience visited on the Reddit and Facebook social networks. Then they launched the beta version testing program and encouraged people to register on their landing page. To apply to the beta version testing program, people had not only to register, but also to introduce their project and write a motivation message explaining why they should be selected. The Pisound team post on Reddit looked like this:

> For those who are into Raspberry Pi based audio projects, this may be of interest. Guys from Blokas Labs are developing an Audio / MIDI interface for RPI and what's best - they are looking for beta testers! It's a little board equipped with 24-bit

192kHz Stereo I/O and MIDI Din-5 I/O ports. Just visit their site for more info: http://blokas.io Cheers!

Out of all the people who registered, the Pisound team selected a few to whom they sent prototypes for testing purposes. This strategy allowed the Pisound team not only to attract potential clients, but also to improve their product. They received important feedback and learned about new examples of how their product could be used.

Let me remind you: something that works for some people will be completely ineffective for others. Never trust a single strategy. Try to experiment and see what works the best for you.

LANDING PAGE

The above-mentioned strategies highlight the importance of collecting potential backers' contact details. Why is this important nowadays, when everyone uses social networks? Maybe it is better to gather people in a specially created Facebook group?

Sadly, social networks are not enough, because there is no guarantee that your followers will see your post. It can get lost in the endless flow of the other information everyone sees on their Facebook news feed. The data published by Hubspot shows that every Facebook post organically (i.e. with no additional advertising) attracts only about 2–6% fans' attention (and the more there are, the lower the reach is). In addition, Facebook is constantly promoting the purchase of paid advertisements, and as a result of its recent algorithm update, organic reachability has dropped dramatically.

Just to compare, the average open rate of a newsletter is 25%. That is a few times higher than the reach of a Facebook post. So in order to increase your influence and reach people interested in your project more effectively, you need their email addresses. Having said that, you can then actively communicate with them by sending relevant information.

To gather the contact details of people you are acquainted with is quite simple—all you have to do is write a message to them on Facebook and ask for their email address. But if you want to massively gather other people's contacts, the method you should be using is a special website page known as a *squeeze page* or *landing page*. Unlike other web pages, the squeeze page is designed to get the visitor's email address.

These are the main elements of the squeeze page:

1. Compelling headline with unique selling proposition (USP),
2. Image or video showing context of your product in use,
3. User reviews or another social proof that enhances reliability,
4. Benefits for your users,
5. Call to action (CTA).

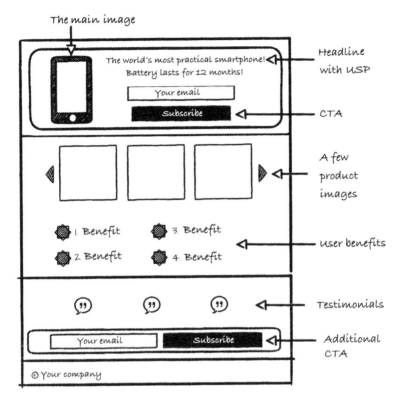

Fig. 24. Squeeze page structure

Unique Selling Proposition (USP)

It is said that a user decides whether to stay on a website or leave it within three seconds. Your task is to present something that will interest and make the user not just stay longer, but to also leave their email address. That is why a USP is necessary.

It is a short text that shows how your product is different and answers the question: *Why should the user care?* The USP shouldn't lead to immediate purchase, but it should make the user curious to learn more about your product. We've already spoken about the *funnel*, so a compelling headline with USP should push your potential consumers down the *buying funnel*. A landing page can be treated as a funnel as well, which means that user should be encouraged to scroll the website, read product benefits, user reviews and, ultimately, leave their contact details.

Almost every day, without even realizing it, we are faced with incentives to do some kind of action. Take note that before you open an article, you first read the headline that aims to interest and encourage action. I'm sure you've heard the term *click-bait headlines* that are meant to exploit the *curiosity gap*, providing just enough information to make readers curious, but not enough to satisfy their curiosity without clicking through to the linked content. Have you ever wondered what words or images led you to a click on a link?

Lots of well-known brands have slogans that encourage users to choose them. One of the most known slogans belongs to Domino's Pizza: "Fresh, hot pizza delivered in 30 minutes or less or it's free." The user is promised to be delivered a fresh and warm pizza within 30 minutes, and if the company fails to do that, the client gets it for free. Another example is the Burger King slogan that was designed to compete with McDonalds: "Have it your way." It is emphasized that everything is in the hands of the client who can choose ingredients for their meal according to their personal needs. The last example belongs to the car rental company Avis, who just could not surpass their main competitor—Hertz. Avis therefore decided to turn their weakness into an advantage with this slogan: "We're number two. We try harder." With this, they emphasize that they are always trying harder because of their placement.

What unites all of these examples? In order to create a good slogan, all the companies mentioned here had to get a good understanding of the problems of their target audience, their strengths and weaknesses, and have knowledge of their competitors. One of the ways to create a good USP is to analyze these three elements: What does your target audience want? What are your competitors doing right? and What makes you different?

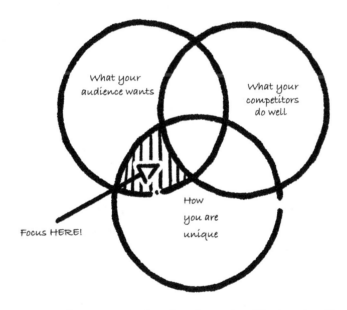

Fig. 25. Identifying your USP based on the needs of the target audience, the strengths of the competitors, and your distinctive features

We have already discussed the topic of your target audience, which is why we will assume here that you already know your clients, what problems they encounter, and what their needs are. So it is time to get to know your competitors and find out your distinctive features. You can find competitors by analyzing similar crowdfunding campaigns, by searching on Google, by using SimilarWeb or other tools that allow you to find similar websites, or by communicating with your target audience. When you make your competitor list, explore their websites. What is their publicly declared USP? What distinctive features do they emphasize?

After finding out your competitors' USP, think about how you are different. You have to find a specific niche that will resonate with the problems of your target audience. It is even better if the exclusivity is delivered as if it were formulated by your client. In order to achieve this, take note of the words and phrases that your target audience uses on social networks, discussions, or when they are writing emails. Your USP has to be short, clear, and understandable in a few seconds. Here are some examples of different USPs of campaigns presented on Kickstarter:

1. **Pico—Craft Beer at Home.** Brew your own fresh, personalized craft beer using professional equipment and ingredients from a worldwide BrewMarketplace. Uniqueness—the possibility to brew fresh beer at home, by using ingredients from local brewers around the world.

2. **B-2 Nano Blade—World's Smallest Tactical Pocket Knife.** Best concealed carry pocket knife for everyday carry. Uniqueness—the smallest tactical pocket knife in the world with a

lifetime guarantee.

3. **Wiivv—World's First Custom Fit Sandals for Personalized Comfort**. Custom fit sandals that are digitally mapped from your smartphone. Uniqueness—the world's first custom fit sandals made with a three-dimensional printer.

Have you noticed some similarities between two of the above-mentioned USPs? When I spoke to Adomas, a guy who helped eight Kickstarter campaigns to raise over a million dollars, he said that when choosing a global USP it should fit to the following phrase: "The world's first xyz," where the xyz is your product's distinctiveness. As you can see, two of the products above used this formulation rule.

Image (The Hero Shot)

Nowadays, a text-only USP is not enough, so it is necessary to add an image or video of your product, or your customer interacting with your product. The best option is to add a high-quality product photo, but if you don't have the product ready yet, a prototype visualization will be enough. Sometimes, a short video clip is uploaded instead of a photo or after it, which gives more information to the user about the issues that the product solves, its use cases, and its exclusivity. A properly selected hero shot reinforces the headline and USP of your landing page.

User Benefits

After getting the interest of a visitor, you can provide more information about how the product you offer will solve their problems. This may be a list of features and their benefits to the user, which will explain the value and exclusivity of your product. Do not overdo the description of the value—write in a concise and clear way, and illustrate the benefits with appropriate icons.

Social Proof (User Reviews, Testimonials, Endorsements)

Imagine yourself as a potential backer of your own project and try to guess what thoughts come to the users' minds. Rarely do people want to be a guinea pig, which is why many consumers need social proof before purchasing a product. Social proof is a variety of reviews from friends, acquaintances, or prominent people in social networks and forums. All of this increases their confidence in a particular brand and gives the user a sense of security.

The best guarantee of reliability is positive feedback from users. To get real reviews, you can start a beta tester program, as the Pisound team did. If the product is ready and the cost of it is relatively low, you can send samples to influencers (we'll talk about them in this chapter) to try out your products and share their experience with you and their followers. But what if you have only one or two prototypes, and these are extremely expensive? In this case, you can request that feedback be written by the first users available. If you have enough resources, present your prototype at an exhibition and suggest people try your product. Carefully listen to their opinions and ask them if you can film them. A video or a picture of a person who has given a review will reinforce their testimonial and make it more personalized.

User reviews are not the only thing that increases reliability. You have most likely seen companies flaunting their certificates or awards on their websites. Just putting up these badges creates a kind of confidence. So do not miss out on contests that suit your product and declare your achievements publicly. If you do not have any certificates or awards, share one of your previous success stories. This way, you will show that you have had success previously, and that will allow your followers to believe in your success this time as well.

Another method, most likely the most effective, is to get in contact with influencers and make them interested in your project so you can get their recommendation. Famous people have a lot of followers, so by receiving their positive feedback, you will be able to enhance your project's reliability. Finally, do not forget the press. It is one of the main means of forming a public opinion. We will talk more in this chapter about how to get in contact with influencers and interest journalists, so they will post an article about you.

Last piece of advice: do not overdo it when trying to build trust because excessive information on the site may be distracting and reduce the likelihood of a visitor's conversion.

Call to Action

If you have managed to interest a visitor, they see value in your idea, and they trust you, all that is left is to encourage them to take the last step—leave their email address. Internet marketers often refer to a *call to action* by its acronym: CTA. This is a generic term that describes any action that your potential customer could take, with the help of your encouragement. It can be an incentive to click on a link, leave an email address, fill in a form, or reply to an email.

When creating a website to gather potential backers (your squeeze page), it is usual to encourage visitors to leave their email by offering product discounts (early bird prices) or telling that they will be the first to know when project is launched. You can also offer a trial version of the product, an ebook, a case study, an infographic, a consultation, discount coupons, industry overview, video material, a free seminar, training course, etc. There are no limits for what you can offer in exchange for their email. Here's an example from the Millo landing page, where they offer a simple call to action—reserve a Millo blender.

World's quietest & most convenient blender

Imagine a smoothie maker that will not wake up your loved ones and takes only 5 seconds to be washed. Starting at only £299.

Fig. 26. Call to action on the Millo landing page

The structure of an incentive to leave an email address is usually the following:

- text (a brief explanation of what the visitor will receive);
- picture (it is not necessary, but graphics usually increase the conversion rate);
- a form to leave their email, or a button that links to the form.

Fig. 27. An example of a call to action (CTA)

If you want to find out more or see more examples, type the keyword "lead magnet" into a search engine. A lead magnet is a valuable offer (usually free of charge) to visitors of the website, and is provided in exchange for contact details (usually an email address).

By the way, I'm sure you've seen a pop-up window that appears a few seconds after visiting a site. This window is also a good example of a lead magnet. Users are usually annoyed by it, but statistics show, that websites that use pop-up windows gather far more contacts than websites without them.

Platforms for Creating Landing Page

Probably the most popular platform for creating websites is WordPress. One of the easiest ways to create a landing page is to buy a ready-to-use WordPress theme. If you enter "one-page product landing page" or "single page product landing page" into the search engine, you will find many places to get such themes. One portal which I personally use for ready-to-use themes is ThemeForest.

First, you need to review available themes by entering the right keyword that describes your need, e.g. "product launch," "product page," "book page," etc. On the right side, you'll see the price of this theme, number of reviews, how many themes are sold, and when it was last updated. You can also check the demo of the theme you like and see how it looks and feels. These themes are not unique, but you can get them at a relatively low price ($29–$69).

Before purchasing a WordPress template, you'll need two things: a server hosting service and a domain name. Usually, you can purchase them from the same service provider. When you have access to your server, you can install WordPress. It is easy and doesn't require any programming skills. One last thing before buying a theme is to check which WordPress version it is compatible with. Avoid outdated versions, as you may experience problems in the future. Once that is checked, you can purchase a theme and upload it on your WordPress website. Do not worry: each theme will have detailed documentation on how to make it ready.

After uploading the website template, you will have to upload the pictures, text, and connect the newsletter program. Even though knowledge of programming is not necessary, some skills are required. Some people enjoy learning new things and prefer to do this by themselves, so if you're one of them, you'll easily find all the answers in search engines. But if you don't want to waste your time and prefer to focus on other things which bring more value, just hire a freelancer who will do all this work for you. You can find such people on UpWork, Freelancer, Guru, or Fiverr.

Despite the familiarity and simplicity of WordPress, there are currently a number of tools (Instapage, LeadPages, Unbounce, ClickFunnels, etc.) that make life even easier and allow you to create a website for collecting contacts even faster. Unlike in the case described above, you will not need to move the template to the server and learn WordPress subtleties. You just choose the right layout for your website and add your own photos and text. All this is done using a user-friendly interface that allows you to simply drag and drop the required text or photo blocks from one place to another. These platforms are convenient because they have all the required plugins:

- forms for gathering contacts,
- integration with social networks (Facebook, Twitter, Instagram, etc.) and newsletter programs (Mailchimp, ConvertKit, GetResponse, etc.),
- A/B testing and other analytics,
- a big variety of templates,
- compatibility with all devices (laptops, tablets, and smartphones).

Is everything as beautiful as it sounds? No. I admit that this method is simpler than creating a website with WordPress templates, but after trying this myself, I missed the flexibility of being able to change some parameters and the overall structure. I tried to find an answer, but the documentation wasn't so detailed, compared to what you can find if you face an issue with WordPress. So, personally, I would go ahead with the first option, because for me, it is more flexible and more cost-effective when looking at the long term.

Landing page building platforms declare that users do not need any programming skills, but that does not mean that you will not need other skills. Things will not move the way you expect if you cannot find the right template or improve it in one way or another. Then you might start getting stuck in exactly the same way as when configuring a WordPress site. In this case, you should just delegate this work to a professional. However, if you find a layout which looks good and doesn't require any changes, landing page platforms can be a great choice.

Website Search Engine Optimization

One of the ways to attract your target audience is website search engine optimization (SEO). First, you will have to work out the right keywords for your product. Then you'll have to periodically post useful content on news portals, blogs, social networks, and directories, with backlinks to your website and perform other actions that will help build your website ranking. If you appear higher on search engines, more people will visit your website.

However, SEO is rather a long-term strategy and will not bring significant results in the short term. If you have to launch a Kickstarter campaign in just a few months, forget this method. SEO is worth choosing when you have a long-term vision and plan to develop your project anyway, regardless of the results of your Kickstarter campaign.

The SEO process takes time and effort. If you want to consolidate traffic and maintain your position, you have to work on it constantly, and pay the person or company responsible for this type of work. Will it pay off? I do not know. It all depends on the funds you are planning to spend on SEO, how many potential clients will be attracted, their conversion rate, your product profit margin, and other things. Just as in previously mentioned methods, SEO can also be assigned to the funnel principle. You can monitor and improve it with the help of Google Analytics.

One of the parts of SEO is to constantly create relevant content by using important keywords. In order to evaluate whether this method suits you, I suggest conducting an experiment. By using Google, try to find an article on the topic of your project. If articles in the first page of results are short and non-informative, and the design of the website has not changed since the 2000s, that is a good opportunity for you to shine. Write an article that is a few times better, more informative, has text that reflects today's issues, and add some graphics. You do not need to write the content yourself; you can just create the structure, specify the sources of information, and give this job to a copywriter.

Once you have the content ready, spread it around relevant blogs and websites. You can find them by using keyword analysis tools or backlink checkers of existing articles that you want to compete with. You do not need to upload the content to your blog. You can make a *guest post* to some blog or contribute to a news portal. Another way is to share it on social networks, such as *LinkedIn*, as it allows you to post articles or content sharing platforms (e.g. *Medium*). Whatever option you choose, it is important to leave a link to your site in the article so that interested people would be redirected to your landing page and Google's algorithm would index the backlink.

If content creation doesn't interest you but you know a certain area well, you can actively participate (ask questions, answer, and assist other members) in relevant forums, social networking groups, or special platforms (Quora, Reddit). If you do not want to do this either, you can share other content created by adding your own comment (for example, you can take interesting statistics from a particular article and submit an infographic to your followers on social networks). Since the goal is the same—directing interested visitors to your site—you can try Sniply (https://snip.ly). This tool allows you to create a special link to any article, and your referring visitors will see a special form for them to leave their email, or a button linking to your website when reading this article.

However, SEO is rather a long-term strategy and will not bring significant results in the short term. If you have to launch a Kickstarter campaign in just a few months, forget this method. SEO is worth choosing when you have a long-term vision and plan to develop your project anyway, regardless of the results of your Kickstarter campaign.

The SEO process takes time and effort. If you want to consolidate traffic and maintain your position, you have to work on it constantly, and pay the person or company responsible for this type of work. Will it pay off? I do not know. It all depends on the funds you are planning to spend on SEO, how many potential clients will be attracted, their conversion rate, your product profit margin, and other things. Just as in previously mentioned methods, SEO can also be assigned to the funnel principle. You can monitor and improve it with the help of Google Analytics.

One of the parts of SEO is to constantly create relevant content by using important keywords. In order to evaluate whether this method suits you, I suggest conducting an experiment. By using Google, try to find an article on the topic of your project. If articles in the first page of results are short and non-informative, and the design of the website has not changed since the 2000s, that is a good opportunity for you to shine. Write an article that is a few times better, more informative, has text that reflects today's issues, and add some graphics. You do not need to write the content yourself; you can just create the structure, specify the sources of information, and give this job to a copywriter.

Once you have the content ready, spread it around relevant blogs and websites. You can find them by using keyword analysis tools or backlink checkers of existing articles that you want to compete with. You do not need to upload the content to your blog. You can make a *guest post* to some blog or contribute to a news portal. Another way is to share it on social networks, such as *LinkedIn*, as it allows you to post articles or content sharing platforms (e.g. *Medium*). Whatever option you choose, it is important to leave a link to your site in the article so that interested people would be redirected to your landing page and Google's algorithm would index the backlink.

If content creation doesn't interest you but you know a certain area well, you can actively participate (ask questions, answer, and assist other members) in relevant forums, social networking groups, or special platforms (Quora, Reddit). If you do not want to do this either, you can share other content created by adding your own comment (for example, you can take interesting statistics from a particular article and submit an infographic to your followers on social networks). Since the goal is the same—directing interested visitors to your site—you can try Sniply (https://snip.ly). This tool allows you to create a special link to any article, and your referring visitors will see a special form for them to leave their email, or a button linking to your website when reading this article.

"WARM UP" LEADS

We have discussed a lot of methods of gathering contacts, so now it is time to look at what to do when somebody joins your mailing list. First of all, it is important to understand that a person who has left their email is already interested in your product, but is not ready to support your project yet. A good seller should follow a certain sales process and lead a potential customer toward the goal steadily, instead of immediately trying to sell the product. When you try to push the product immediately, you risk losing a potential backer.

Warming up the potential backers is also called *lead nurturing*. It's a process that helps build a relationship with your potential customers, moving them through the sales funnel towards your goal. In your case, you'll build a bond and strengthen the relationship between your subscribers and you, with the help of a sequence of periodically sent emails. In those emails, you will gradually introduce the prehistory of the project, reveal the main reasons why you started this project, explain the problem that your product solves, and the value that it creates for your backers. Your goal is to engage with your potential customers, make them excited, and motivate them to back your project when launch day comes.

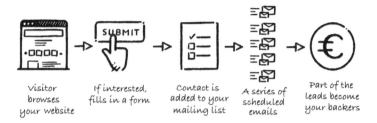

Fig. 28. The process of "warming up" the visitors of your website

The first step is to create 4–5 emails that will later be placed into a newsletter sending program to be sent to your mailing list within a period of 5 to 10 days. At the end of each mail, there should be a hook that will make your subscribers curious and excited to wait for another email. To learn more about creating such an email sequence, I'd recommend reading the book *DotCom Secrets: The Underground Playbook for Growing Your Company Online* by Russell Brunson. He has a dedicated chapter named "The soap opera sequence" where he explains in detail why such emails work, describes their structure, and provides examples of each mail to understand how they are written.

In the first message, you should thank your subscribers for registering and give them a personal greeting. Next, you should give an impression that the addressee will get something special, such as exclusive access that others do not know about. It is also good to mention that more details will be revealed in the coming days, but don't talk about the product itself yet. The first (or "welcome") email is usually sent immediately, as soon as the visitor leaves their email address through your form.

You'll be able to set a rule for how fast the first email should be sent to a new subscriber in your email newsletter program. Here's the first email that was automatically sent to those who left their email on the Millo smart smoothie maker landing page:

> Hi, this is Adam, the founder of Millo
>
> Thank you for signing up. You have just gained exclusive access to the part of Millo that barely anyone knows. I'll introduce it to you in the upcoming days.
>
> A lot of things see this world purely out of someone seeking to benefit.
>
> Millo isn't one of those things. It wasn't born out of one of those times when some random guy thought *That would be a cool product, let's make some money!*
>
> No.
>
> Millo was born with a mission behind it. A dream I aimed towards after the suffering, drama and looking for the purpose in life.
>
> Stay with me and be surprised when I tell you what this is all about.
>
> The first part is out tomorrow. Look for an email with the subject line *Re-connecting to reality.*
>
> Glad to see you here!
>
> Adam

It's important to leave the hook at the end of the email that will interest your subscribers, or create a call to action that will encourage them to answer a specific question, express their opinion, vote for something, click on a link, share something with their friends, and so on. The intrigue must be maintained throughout the whole email sequence.

The second message should start as dramatically as possible. You should tell your hardest life event—a breakthrough that has changed you or the way you think. I know it's not easy to create, write, and share your personal stories with strangers, but remember that your goal is to create a bond between you and your subscribers. You should create an atmosphere so that the reader of your email will equate themself to you and feel commonality. If you manage to do this, you will strengthen the relationship between you and your audience, and a part of the readers will start to like you not for your product (remember that you have not even mentioned it yet in your emails), but for who you are—your personality.

Here's the second email sent to Millo subscribers:

> I was sitting together with my daughter, playing with her, yet I wasn't really there with her. I was merely existing, trying to push through time until I could go to bed.
>
> This didn't just happen once. I was disconnected. Drained by both the everyday life and the fact that I wasn't appreciating the time with my daughter and wife. I was stuck in this loop.
>
> On the outside it looked like I was living the dream and I actually could have. A job I've always wanted, I just became a father and was in a loving relationship.
>
> But really, I wasn't present. My mind was wandering, my energy was low, focusing was hard. Morally - I was in shambles.
>
> Everything was just the status quo. Something I thought I

should be doing in life to appear successful, not the things I actually wanted to do.

Not being present, understanding it and being disappointed in yourself for the very same reasons was draining.

STOP!

This isn't the dad I want to be. This isn't the husband I want to be. This isn't the man I want to be!

This was it, the moment I decided I would change. Starting now.

I didn't know how at the time so I went looking for advice and found some.

Skeptical at first, yet thankful I took the plunge. It all led to things much bigger than I could have imagined, but more about that - tomorrow.

Look for an email with the subject line *Only open if you're ready to start living, not merely existing.*

Yours,

Adam

P.S. What gets you going when stuck in low energy loop? Just reply to this email, I answer them all!

In the third message, you can start talking about the product, by giving more interesting and intriguing information: the main problems of the target audience, how the idea of solving this problem arose, what challenges you encountered in developing a prototype, how the product should change the consumer's daily lives, etc. With the help of these emails, you'll keep in touch with your subscribers until the project launch date comes.

You should keep track of subscribers' engagement and regularly check email open rates, click rates, and responses.

If you start collecting contacts in advance, there may be a time gap between the last message in the automated email sequence and the launch date of your project. In this case, occasionally remind them about your project by sending a newsletter to your mailing list. When you've already set a launch date, remind your subscribers at least two times a week and 24 hours before the start of your campaign. And of course, the most important thing is to send an email when the project is live.

As discussed previously, if you've properly selected the target audience, they were well engaged in your email sequence, and understood the value of your product, you can expect about 2–3% of the people in your mailing list to become your backers. Most of them will back the project in the first days, as they will be encouraged by limited early bird rewards. But in general, it's human nature to procrastinate, so keep sending emails throughout the campaign and you'll see that each letter will have some impact on new backers. Send an email to your subscribers 24 hours after the launch day thanking them for their support, once you reach 100% of your funding goal, or when you decide to introduce a new reward or create stretch goals, etc.

If you want to see more examples of "warming up" letters, register on a few landing pages yourself. Analyze and compare the letters you receive. You may take something you like from each letter and adapt it to your case.

If you want to find out the structure of the letters and find out more about them, aside from *DotCom Secrets: The Underground Playbook for Growing Your Company Online* by Russell Brunson, I recommend reading these books:

- Dan S Kennedy, *The Ultimate Sales Letter: Attract New Customers. Boost your Sales* (the author is a guru of direct response advertising. You will find out why some letters help to sell, and others don't, how to formulate a good headline or the subject of an email, how to use graphic elements, etc.);
- Robert B. Cialdini, *Influence: The Psychology of Persuasion* (amazing book which will help you understand the key principles of influence and you will be able to apply them not only during the preparation of a crowdfunding campaign, but also in other areas of life).

INVOLVE YOUR AUDIENCE

A target audience that is more involved in your project not only has better conversion rates, but also gives more recommendations and useful suggestions on how to improve your product. You can engage with your audience by allowing them to contribute to your product development, express their views on specific issues, vote for the most liked product design or the most needed feature, or answer a questionnaire or survey by giving them the possibility to win a prize.

In my case, I promised to send the book in PDF

format to anyone who would read the manuscript of my book and add written comments or suggestions. Altogether, there were 180 people who filled in a short form and agreed to review the book. I gave them a certain time to go through the manuscript and followed up a few times to ask about their progress. In the end, most of them said there was nothing to add and just a few of them added really useful comments that were taken into consideration.

All this process of giving the potential readers the chance to review the manuscript not only improved the content, but they also felt that I cared about their opinion and used it to make the book better. I did a similar thing by asking them to vote for the cover design, but this time I did not give out any prize. Nevertheless, people actively participated and expressed their opinions, indicating the most-liked cover versions. A side effect was that most of those people who reviewed the book or expressed their opinion on cover design were more active during the Kickstarter campaign.

The creators of Pisound also involved their followers by announcing a beta tester program. Those who wanted to try the product had to register on their site, introduce themselves, and explain the reason why they should be selected. This program got a lot of interest and within 24 hours, Pisound had collected about a thousand registered visitors. Prototypes for testing were sent to the selected people. This strategy served not only as a way of attracting potential customers, but also helped improve the product, as in collaboration with the beta testers, the

Pisound team received a lot of useful feedback and learned new cases of how people used their product.

FACEBOOK ADS

Most creators, especially new ones, dream about free traffic for their campaign, but the truth is that most Kickstarter projects that raise a hundred thousand dollars or more use paid advertisements. Some projects that do not require big funding can be brought to life by using a personal network and other creative methods to attract new backers, but if you see that your methods do not work or you just simply do not want to waste time experimenting, you can use Facebook ads. Even though there are lots of types of online advertising, we will be focusing on a Facebook advertisement for two simple reasons. This social network has a massive audience and it gives you the ability to precisely pick out the people that fit your potential backer profile.

Let's start with the main terms in online advertising that you should know.

- **Reach**—the number of people who have seen your ads within a certain period. This indicator shows the number of people who have seen it, regardless of the number of times the advertisement has been shown to them.
- **Impressions**—the number of times your ads were on screen for your target audience. Different from reach, impressions also include cases where the ad is shown to the same person several times.

- **Cost per thousand impressions (CPM)**—the cost of showing the ad a thousand times.
- **Cost per click (CPC)**—the cost of one click. Pay per click (PPC) is one of the online advertising types where you pay for a click on the ad.
- **Click-through rate (CTR)**—the conversion rate in percentage. It shows what percentage of the people who saw that advertisement then clicked on it. This indicator shows the quality of the ad. If the click-through rate is low, it indicates that your ad set (text or the graphic element) isn't engaging, or that you are showing it to the wrong audience.
- **Cost per lead (CPL)**—the average cost of a potential client's contact (email). Facebook has a special type of advertising—Lead Ads, dedicated to the acquisition of potential clients' contacts. When this type is chosen, Facebook users fill out a special form on the platform itself, without being redirected to the external website. It is convenient for users because they don't need to leave Facebook to fill in their contact details after clicking an ad.
- **Customer acquisition cost (CAC)**—the cost of attracting a new client through advertising. If you know the self-cost of your product and your profit margin, it will be easy for you to calculate how much you can spend on advertising for it to pay off.

Let's make an example. If CPM is $1 and you want to show your ad on Facebook for a million people who belong to your target audience, you should dedicate a budget of $1000 for advertising. Suppose every hundredth one clicked on the ad and a thousand people provided their emails. Then CTR is 1%, CPC is $0.1, and CPL is $1. After warming up your potential backers and sending them through your email sequence, let's say you introduced your Kickstarter campaign and 50 of them supported your product. Then CAC is $20. If one unit of your product is sold for $100 and the self-cost of it is $50, your profit after having subtracted the advertising costs will be 100-50-20 = $30. For every dollar spent on advertising, you receive one and a half. Reminder—this is just an example, so you will know how to evaluate the efficiency of your advertising.

There are different goals of advertising: to attract visitor traffic to the landing page, to acquire registered users, to collect likes, to sell a product or service, etc. As we are talking about preparing for a crowdfunding campaign, we will concentrate on one specific goal—to collect potential backer emails. For this you will need to:

1. Create an account for your project on Facebook;
2. Gather a target audience (you can first set a wide audience by using a geographic location, age, gender, and interests. Later, by observing the advertising results, slowly narrow down the criteria and select several segments, so you can see which brings the best results);
3. Choose a few pictures and write a few text lines that you will use for different ad sets, which will be shown to a selected audience (it is especially important that the ad is oriented to the needs of a specific client because the more people from the target audience engage with the ad and find it

relevant, the less you have to pay for it);
4. Build a landing page for the collection of contacts (this is recommended, but not obligatory, if you decide to use the Lead Ads function on Facebook);
5. Write a series of automated emails to warm up potential backers you have collected.

If you have decided to collect potential backers using Facebook advertising, find out the conversion averages in your area and talk to people who have advertised similar projects (so they will share their experience and figures). However, no information or discussion will be better than own experience and knowledge, which you accumulate independently, while advertising your product.

So, create the first ad yourself. Start with a small budget and pay attention that the essence of advertising efficiency is testing. You probably will not be able to create an ad with good conversion immediately, but with the help of A/B testing, you will find out what is most attractive to your target audience.

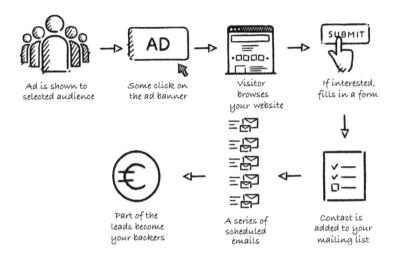

Fig. 29. The collection of potential backers by using Facebook ads

Find the Right Audience with Facebook Advertising

Facebook ads are one of the best methods of determining your audience due to the huge number of users and the ability to do precise segmentation. You can define things like gender, age, geographic location (you can find information about the countries and cities where most backers come from by analyzing the "Community" section of Kickstarter campaigns that are similar to yours), interests, behaviors, etc., while setting who should see your ads. By using the Facebook advertising tool Audience Insights (see Fig. 30) and entering the desired criteria, you will find out how many people that match your audience can be reached using Facebook ads.

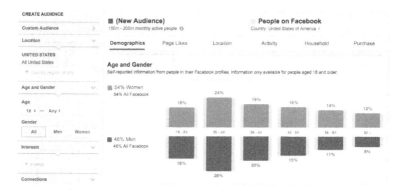

Fig. 30. Audience Insights helps in determining your target audience

You should run A/B tests of the same ad set (image and text) by changing just one element (gender, country, interest, etc.) in your filter. In this way, you will learn which audience engages with your ads better. Then you can narrow your audience and delete those that don't convert and increase your budget for those that convert the best.

Lead Ads

You can either point the visitors from the Facebook ad banner to your landing page or choose an alternative option: Lead Ads. This is very useful if you target people who browse Facebook on their smartphones. By clicking on a Lead Ad, the user does not need to leave Facebook, making it more convenient for them to sign up for your newsletter. Creating a landing page, adding signup forms, integrating it with newsletter programs, and optimizing the site for a better conversion rate takes time and requires investment. That's why Lead Ads is a great option for those who want to collect leads without a landing page.

The only disadvantage is that the ad banner doesn't provide as much information as you would on a website, so someone who has filled in a form after clicking an ad may not be as qualified as the visitor who has checked your website and left his contact details there. But if you select your audience well, run A/B testing with different text and image variations, and create a series of engaging emails, I'm sure you will be able to create a great mailing list for your project.

The Story of SGS Watches

One of the best examples illustrating the efficiency of a Facebook ad strategy is the project SGS Watches, which collected more than $747,000 HKD ($95,229 USD). They chose fairly simple target audience criteria: country—USA (where the most Kickstarter backers reside), age—18–65 years, gender—unimportant, interests—Kickstarter and watches. Here's the ad they used:

SGS Watches
December 22, 2016

The Eagle is the first pilot watch constructed with the same materials as some of the world's most expensive watches, for a fraction of the price.

Launching soon on Kickstarter: https://go.sgswatches.com

Most watch companies use a complicated distribution process that leaves you with a price tag of several thousand dollars. However, we've built a unique system that allows us to remove the middlemen looking for their cut and deliver the watch directly to you, for less than $150.

Don't miss the news: https://go.sgswatches.com

Fig. 31. SGS Watches ad on Facebook

Users who clicked on this message were automatically directed to the squeeze page. The same picture of the SGS Watches and the logo of the company were used on that page, to connect the advertising message and the website (see Fig. 32).

Fig. 32. SGS Watches squeeze page

Every website visitor who left their email was automatically added to the mailing list of potential backers. All of the people from this list received an email sequence five days in a row, at 24-hour intervals. The final email presented a request to support the project. During the pre-launch phase, the SGS Watches team acquired 4000 potential backers and 5% of them supported the project once it was launched on Kickstarter.

SMOKE TESTING

What's the best way to evaluate whether the market needs your product before launching your Kickstarter campaign? Try to sell your product and see if people spend their money on it. I'm sure you'll agree that buying your product before it's even created is the best metric to see if your product has a demand. This method is called *smoke testing* and to run it, you need to create a website for your product, where people can actually make a purchase.

First, you'll need to have a website ready and optimize it to achieve a good conversion rate for simple email signups. Run a few A/B tests with different versions of your landing page and see which one converts better. Then, for a week or two, drive some traffic to your site by running highly targeted Facebook ads. Some website visitors will sign up and their contact details will automatically go to your mailing list. Once you have at least a few hundred leads, you can send them an email by saying that they can be the first to pre-order your product. Point them to your website with a simulated checkout process. Before visitors enter their credit card details, they should see a message like this: "You are too late—products are out of stock." Of course, you may actually accept their money and then send a refund, explaining that you were trying to evaluate market reaction. Both options are suitable, so choose whichever you like.

After your smoke test is finished, you can analyze your results: the click-through-rate (CTR) for your ads, clicks on a link after you sent an email, and the overall conversion rate of website visitors who completed a purchase process. This data is very important, as you can use it to predict how many leads you will need to reach your goal on Kickstarter.

The creators of Millo ran a smoke test before launching their Kickstarter campaign. They managed to sell just one item of their product. That's not impressive, but one is still better than zero. There's a probability that no one will make a purchase during your smoke test. This doesn't mean you don't have a product/market fit, but it's a strong signal that something is wrong and maybe you haven't figured out your target audience yet.

PRE-LAUNCH FUNNEL

Marketing and sales processes are usually described using the *funnel* analogy. It works for systemizing your preparation for a crowdfunding campaign as well. In this case, the funnel is split into several parts: the top is the collection of target audience contacts (leads), and at the bottom is them supporting the project. Some of the people whose contacts you have collected, when moving through the funnel towards the goal, will lose their interest (will be sieved) for various reasons at each stage, and some will complete all stages (will become your backers or clients).

The transition from one stage to the next is called the *conversion*. By looking at your funnel, you can see the number of leads in each stage and calculate the conversion rate. Peter Drucker, author and one of the greatest management consultants and educators, said: "If you can't measure it, you can't improve it." So as long as you can measure the number of leads in each stage, you can improve your results.

Let's analyze an example of a pre-launch funnel (Fig. 33). In the first stage, the traffic is directed to a squeeze page. You can drive traffic to your page from your social networks, newsletters, by posting in forums, groups, or other niche websites that your target audience uses, or by running online ads.

For sure, not everyone will click on the link you share and just a portion of those who see your post will click the link and will visit your website (stage 2). You will be able to monitor the number of visitors on your website after installing Google Analytics. Some visitors will be interested in your idea and will leave their contact details (stage 3). By leaving their contact details, they agree to receive news about your product and other relevant information. This condition is usually written in small print and sounds like this: *By clicking Sign up, I agree to the Terms of Use and Privacy Policy.*

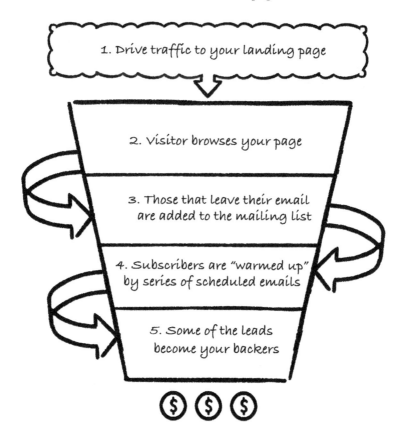

Fig. 33. An example funnel for the preparation of a crowdfunding campaign

The landing page needs to be optimized so that a higher percentage of visitors will leave their contact details. We've already covered A/B testing, which is one of the optimization methods. By observing what elements are the most worthwhile and making appropriate changes in your website, you will be to generate leads more efficiently, at a minimal cost. This part is very important as lead price determines your client acquisition cost.

After visitors leave their email addresses, they will be automatically included in your potential backers list (you'll create this list in your newsletter platform) and will periodically receive emails (that will be fully automated) about your story: how was the idea born, why you decided to bring it to life, what problem you are trying to solve, etc. The purpose of such an email series is to interest your potential backers and show that behind all of this is a simple person who has goals and ambitions, just like any of them.

It's important not only to gather subscribers but also to engage with them and touch them emotionally. You can evaluate their engagement by reviewing statistics in your newsletter platform: responses, open rates, and clicks. Some of the subscribers will unsubscribe, but the remaining ones, after having overcome this process (stage 4), will become more interested potential backers. After introducing the project and informing your mailing list, a portion of them will back your idea (stage 5). Is it possible to predict the percentage of potential backers that become actual backers? Let's discuss some real examples.

CONVERSION RATES

After evaluating the statistics of various Kickstarter projects, it can be assumed that about 2–3% of the gathered potential backers will back your project if you have a good product/market fit and you were able to reach your target audience. In this case, we are not including relatives, friends, or acquaintances, but people who knew nothing about you before becoming part of the potential backers list.

Let's say that your goal is to get $10,000 funding and you are planning to sell your product for $100 per unit. To reach your goal, you need to sell 100 units throughout the campaign. If we make the assumption that 2% of potential backers preorder your product, then in order to reach your goal, you need 100*100/2 = 5,000 potential backers. If you use a higher conversion rate in the formula or make the assumption that some backers will buy a few units, the number of potential backers required decreases.

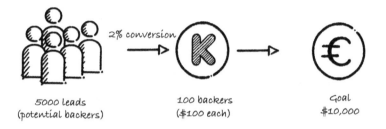

5000 leads (potential backers)   100 backers ($100 each)   Goal $10,000

Fig. 34. The relationship between potential backers and the goal

Case #1: My First Book—10% Conversion

Before starting my *How to Start a VoIP Business* book campaign on Kickstarter, I had a list of around 2,000 business and personal contacts. Those were the people who already knew me and had agreed to be informed when the project was launched.

At that point, I had no idea how many of them would become project backers. This project is now finished, and thus I can share this indicator. In my case, it was

200/2,000 = 10%. Why was my conversion rate a few times higher in comparison to the average 2–3%? First of all, I gathered my contacts naturally, without any advertisements, so these people already knew and trusted me. A long-term relationship and trust increases the chance of them backing your project. As a result, your personal and business contacts will convert much better than those who don't know who you are.

The cost of your product is no less important: the cheaper it is, the faster and more spontaneously your project will be backed. My book cost $25 and that is why potential backers could make a pledge without thinking too much about it.

Case #2: Pisound—7% Conversion

During the preparation period, the Pisound team gathered 2,000 contacts without spending a penny on advertising. They announced that they were looking for beta testers in Reddit and Facebook groups, and people started to register on their landing page organically. After the Pisound campaign was launched, more than 7% became backers. You have to agree: that is an impressive number, considering that the standard for this area is roughly 2–3%! I think that is a perfect example for people who want to bring their idea to life with minimal financial resources.

Case #3: SGS Watches—5% Conversion

After consulting with other project authors, Emilis Strimaitis, the co-founder of the SGS Watches project, got the impression that approximately 2–4% of people from the list would become backers. But Emilis, together with the team, decided to lower their expectations and anticipated that after introducing the SGS Watches project, this indicator would be 1.5–2%.

After calculating and evaluating the cost of attracting one lead through a Facebook advertisement, they decided that this 1.5–2% pessimistic scenario was satisfactory. Once the project was launched, the results exceeded all expectations: the project was backed by 5% of the potential backers. Of course, the whole team was very excited and told that if they could go back in time, they would have invested much more in pre-launch, as conversion rates during the campaign were far from what they achieved with the pre-launch mailing list.

Case #4: Publishing Project—0.5% Conversion

This is a great example that things may not go as well as expected. I was a collaborator in this project and we tried Facebook Ads to generate leads. We were using two options of advertising: lead ads and directing people to the landing page.

"Lead ads" means that a person who finds the ad relevant can leave their contact details (usually name and email or just email address) directly in Facebook after clicking an ad. It's a great option for a few reasons. First, you may generate leads without having a landing page that takes time and effort to build. Second, the price per lead may be lower because a person who's interested in the ad doesn't need to leave Facebook.

In regular Facebook ads, a person clicks the ad, which redirects them to the landing page. Then they need to fill in a form on that website and leave their contact details. Finally, if this site uses *double opt-in*, the person needs to check their email and click the confirmation link that they receive from this website. Just think about how many extra steps there are, and that in each step, this person may change their mind. On the other hand, people that go through the whole process, review the landing page, and confirm that they want to be notified about this project are more qualified and their conversion rates should be higher. So, I'd recommend testing both ad options and choosing the one that brings better results for you.

The first sign that something was wrong was a relatively low open rate. Initially it was around 25%, but in all further emails, the open rate decreased even more. On the launch date, the mailing list had 2,900 subscribers and email open rate was just 15%. In the end, just 0.5% of potential backers in the mailing list became project backers.

Thinking about the reasons for this, there might have been a few. First, leads were collected with the goal of testing Facebook ads and evaluating the price per lead. There was no email sequence, so those leads didn't receive any welcome email. As a result, over time they became "colder" and may have forgotten that they had subscribed. The second reason was the wrong target audience. The book we presented was a luxury and the price of it started at $150, and there's a chance that most of the collected leads were simply not able to afford that. Targeting a higher-income audience was a change made only in the middle of the project.

The moral of this story is that the real result can be completely different from what you may expect. So be prepared for different scenarios.

Case #5: Monimoto—Zero Conversions

This example is probably the worst-case scenario. When preparing to introduce his Monimoto crowdfunding campaign, Andrew, with the help of Google and Facebook advertisements, gathered 400 potential clients. Unfortunately, after introducing his idea, not a single one became a backer...

Sometimes, all the time and money you have invested may just be in vain. You have to accept the risk and understand that when you are preparing for a campaign, there will be a lot of uncertainties which you will not be able to control.

Conclusion

In terms of conversions, I recommend foreseeing a few possible scenarios. The worst one is that the time and investments you have made will bring zero results. It will still allow you to evaluate the demand for your idea and consider if it is worth improving it, or whether it is better to start something new. The second one is that a percentage of your potential backers will support you. You can estimate the preliminary percentage based on examples provided in this book or after having communicated with authors of similar projects. The best scenario is that real results will exceed all expectations. In this case, all that will be left to do is celebrate. After foreseeing the different scenarios, you will be able to preliminarily evaluate how many potential clients need to be collected to reach your goal.

MEDIA OUTREACH

So far, we have only talked about how to get potential backers. But what if we were able to interest journalists whose articles reach thousands or hundreds of thousands of readers, who meet the criteria of your target audience? In this chapter, you will learn how you can interest journalists or bloggers who write about topics related to your project, so they will write an article about your product.

Become an Information Source for a Journalist

Every journalist or blogger is always looking for news on their target topics, expert insights, research, and other information, so they can write the next interesting article. HARO (Help A Reporter) was created exactly for this purpose and it connects professionals and specialists (sources) with journalists.

It has been said that 55,000 journalists and bloggers are registered on the site additionally with 800,000 information suppliers. The principle of operation is simple: journalists create a post with a headline and a short description, to describe what they are looking for, while the suppliers of information subscribe to get notifications about the topics (such as high technologies, travelling, business, finance, etc.) that are relevant to them. After reviewing new requests from journalists, they can get in touch directly via email.

After having tried this tool out, the first thing I noticed was that there were a lot of requests and to get through all of the headlines every day takes about 20–30 minutes. I was subscribed to the news for approximately two weeks, but I never found a story for which I could have created value. I also noticed that the platform is oriented to the US market, so if your topics of expertise are local to other places, they will not be very relevant to journalists on this site.

HARO is not the only site for finding out what kind of stories journalists need right now. You can also use Twitter by entering hashtags such as #journorequest, #PRrequest, or #bloggerrequest. These hashtags will help you to find journalists and bloggers who are looking for information sources or experts. The drawback is that all these requests will be from different areas, unfiltered, so reviewing all of them will take a lot of time.

Create a List of Suitable Journalists

If you use HARO or hashtags, your contact with media begins only when your product and expertise matches a journalist's request. This might suit for a long-term strategy, but it is not effective in crowdfunding pre-launch, as you are short on time and your topic may never show up, or the article will interest very few people who will not have influence on the campaign. So I suggest trying out an alternative—directly contacting journalists, bloggers, or influential people who are relevant to your topic.

You can look for influential people by using special tools or searching. One of the most popular tools designed for this, BuzzSumo, allows you to find the most influential people in your niche and content that use your keywords and are shared the most on social media. Other tools that help to find the most relevant journalists are: Muck Rack, Anewstip, JustReachOut and Hey Press. These tools are all paid, so it is worth starting with a trial version first. Preparation for a crowdfunding campaign is a limited-time job, so a trial period may be enough to find the needed journalists.

Even though the listed tools save your time, they are more appropriate to those who look for journalists and relevant topics every day. In our case, we only have to find journalists once, so you can choose an alternative path—manual research. First of all, you have to analyze successful campaigns similar to yours (see the chapter "Analysis of similar campaigns"). Having found relevant articles that cover stories related to those campaigns, identify the author of these articles. Most often you'll find the journalist's full name at the top or at the end of the article. Create a list of such contacts—if the content isn't too old, they are likely to be interested in the niche of your project.

Creating a list of relevant journalists takes time, so you should set some goal and decide how many contacts you plan to collect. I suggest having at least 200 contacts relevant to your project's area. From a longlist, you should also be able to pick your top 20 shortlist of journalists. You should give more attention to the shortlist (follow them on social media, comment on their articles, try different methods to get in touch) and automate your outreach for the longlist.

Here is a sample list of journalists (see Table 3), sorted by the media outlet's website placement in the world by visitor traffic (I used SimilarWeb to evaluate the website global rankings).

Global Rank	Country	Media Outlet	Full Name	Email
124	USA	bbc.com	Leo Kelion	
132	UK	dailymail.co.uk	Sophie Haslett	
145	USA	buzzfeed.com	Hannah Mars	
154	UK	theguardian.com	Samuel Gibbs	
155	USA	nytimes.com	Courtney Rubin	
187	USA	cnet.com	Andrew Gebhart	
191	USA	huffingtonpost.com	Erin Schumaker	

Table 3. Example list of journalists

Website Global Rank

Website global rank is important, because it shows the weight of a specific portal in the global context. Another fairly popular parameter is domain authority, which shows the placement of the website in search engines. The value of the domain can vary from 1 to 100—the higher the number, the better the result in search engines. Mozrank is one more indicator, which shows the number of links on a website and their quality. This indicator can vary from 0 to 9.99, which means the more links from other pages there are, the higher the Mozrank will be. These and other similar ratings will help you evaluate which journalists should be in your shortlist. But will this really have the biggest influence on the campaign?

The main advantage of the biggest media outlets with a high rating (Huffington Post, TechCrunch, Business Insider, BBC, Forbes, etc.) is that they attract massive traffic and reach a large audience. Also, when they post an article, it soon appears on many smaller blogs, which aggregate relevant information and share it with their readers. So if you're able to get attention of a journalist from The New York Times, Mashable, or TechCrunch, you may not even need to contact the rest—the news will spread on its own.

Of course, there are two sides of the coin. Just because the article is published on a large portal does not mean you will instantly receive huge visitor traffic to your project. There's a chance that you will not receive any attention because it can be drowned out by the large number of other articles. Because of this, you should not forget the importance of social media, specialized blogs, and newsletters. It is highly likely that you will receive better results after having published the news about the project on a local blog, on social media, or after having sent out newsletters.

So when making a list of potential journalists and bloggers, pay attention to niche portals, whose authors care about the topics and are small enough to care about you, but large enough to be worthwhile for you. Maybe, by talking to an author of a blog, you will convince them to share the information about your project on social media or a newsletter. Also, before asking for a favor, become a follower of the portal and subscribe to their newsletter, because you will be able to get to know their style and find out if they are suitable for your project.

Become Acquainted with Journalists Before the Start of the Project

Many creators have just a couple of months to prepare for a project launch. Even though this may seem a rather short time to create a relationship with journalists, it is entirely possible.

If you want to effectively communicate with people who work in news media, you have to first understand what this communication looks like from their point of view. The BuzzStream portal performed a survey of 500 writers, editors, and journalists, wanting to assess the real daily routine of these people. What do you think: how many pitches to write an article about a specific startup, company, or project do the journalists receive every day? Almost half of the respondents receive at least 20 daily requests, but only publish one article per day. If a journalist is more well known or works at a prominent portal, the number of requests per day usually exceeds a hundred! As you see, there's a direct correlation between the authority of a journalist and the number of emails they receive in their inbox each day.

Only 11% of the respondents said that they often write articles about a story they receive from an unknown person. Nevertheless, you can keep hoping, due to the fact that 45% of these authors publish these articles *sometimes*. So your story may still see the light of day.

To increase your chances of getting published in the media, you should first analyze the situation and send ideas only to journalists who write about relevant topics and who could certainly be interested in your story. Check if the person you are going to contact has ever written about a Kickstarter or Indiegogo project (some journalists do not even bother writing about crowdfunding products in the prototype stage). Before revealing information about your idea, you should create value for the chosen journalist and try to get noticed. You can do this in many ways.

- Read the journalist's articles and comment on them, ask interesting questions, and write out your opinion on the topic.
- If you find an interesting and relevant question on Quora, encourage the selected journalist to share their opinion.
- Provide interesting and valuable material that the journalist could use in their article (this could be exclusive research, data or analysis, the results of a survey, a juicy bit of news, expert insights, an interview with an interesting or famous person, etc.
- If the chosen person is an expert in some specific

area, recommend them to a blog that is looking for interesting people, so they can interview them.

- Write an article on the relevant topic and ask them to express their opinion.
- Enter their name and surname or the topics they cover into Google Alerts to constantly receive alerts and quickly react to them.
- Follow them on social media (most journalists use Twitter) and show attention by commenting, sharing information, or pressing "like."
- Subscribe to their blog's newsletter (if there is one).
- Tell your story so it will awaken emotions, and be engaging and related to the topics they are interested in.
- If the journalist provides advice in their article, use it and then reply about how it helped you and what the results were.
- Write an email to them and ask them questions related to their article (this method is only appropriate when discussing the newest articles).

Be Creative When Reaching Out to Key Journalists

I've spoken to Peter Bowles, co-CEO of Dynamo PR who has shared a case study of "3Doodler" (world's first 3D printing pen) that has raised over $2.3 million in Kickstarter.

Dynamo PR team reached out to key journalists in a unique way by making the journalists themselves the first "3D printed journalists in the world". They "doodled" each journalist's Twitter avatar and their titles logo individually, filming these in time-lapsed videos and creating the final 3D objects to send to each journalist to seed 3Doodler to them and engage the journalist with the idea.

By preparing every detail in advance, reaching out to and pre-briefing journalists with their very own 3Doodles, Dynamo secured key coverage on the day of the Kickstarter launch on Popular Science, TechCrunch, Wired, VentureBeat, The Next Web, Der Spiegel, Huffington Post, Fast Company and Engadget.

If you are able to use your product creatively to approach journalists and engage with them, I can guarantee that you'll be ahead of everyone that are using standard methods of press outreach.

Don't Have Time for Building Relations with a Journalist?

In all of the previously listed cases, time is a necessity which the creators usually lack. If the circle of journalist is small—only a couple of dozen, it is possible to create value before contacting them. But if there are several hundred of them, it can be too difficult to do this, so you should select only a couple of main journalists (a shortlist), to whom you will give most of your attention. You will have to contact the rest of them (your longlist) in a simpler way: send them a personalized message first and then several follow up letters. We will discuss this in more detail in this chapter.

One great example that I've heard on how to get your story published without building a relationship first belongs to Gediminas, the creator of Rubbee, the electric drive for bicycles. When I interviewed Gediminas, he told me that he did not even network with journalists in advance. Instead, he spent that time building a list of relevant journalists and creating personalized letters. Once the Rubbee campaign was launched on Kickstarter, he sent those personalized pitches to journalists from his list and told them that they would be the first to have written about Rubbee.

And it worked! Maybe it turned out to work because it was 2013 and, in those days, journalists just did not receive so many letters about Kickstarter projects as they do now? Maybe the creator of Rubbee got lucky? Or maybe he just did everything properly: he presented a unique product, made a list of suitable journalists, and created an intriguing subject and content in each letter?

This story just shows us that there is no secret sauce—everyone finds their own way to success. By the way, Gediminas launched his second Kickstarter project Rubbee X four years later, in 2017. As he had already established contact with press during his first project, this helped to get media attention for the second project, as the press loves follow up stories on something they've covered before and that have achieved significant growth or improvement since then.

first "3D printed journalists in the world". They "doodled" each journalist's Twitter avatar and their titles logo individually, filming these in time-lapsed videos and creating the final 3D objects to send to each journalist to seed 3Doodler to them and engage the journalist with the idea.

By preparing every detail in advance, reaching out to and pre-briefing journalists with their very own 3Doodles, Dynamo secured key coverage on the day of the Kickstarter launch on Popular Science, TechCrunch, Wired, VentureBeat, The Next Web, Der Spiegel, Huffington Post, Fast Company and Engadget.

If you are able to use your product creatively to approach journalists and engage with them, I can guarantee that you'll be ahead of everyone that are using standard methods of press outreach.

Don't Have Time for Building Relations with a Journalist?

In all of the previously listed cases, time is a necessity which the creators usually lack. If the circle of journalist is small—only a couple of dozen, it is possible to create value before contacting them. But if there are several hundred of them, it can be too difficult to do this, so you should select only a couple of main journalists (a shortlist), to whom you will give most of your attention. You will have to contact the rest of them (your longlist) in a simpler way: send them a personalized message first and then several follow up letters. We will discuss this in more detail in this chapter.

One great example that I've heard on how to get your story published without building a relationship first belongs to Gediminas, the creator of Rubbee, the electric drive for bicycles. When I interviewed Gediminas, he told me that he did not even network with journalists in advance. Instead, he spent that time building a list of relevant journalists and creating personalized letters. Once the Rubbee campaign was launched on Kickstarter, he sent those personalized pitches to journalists from his list and told them that they would be the first to have written about Rubbee.

And it worked! Maybe it turned out to work because it was 2013 and, in those days, journalists just did not receive so many letters about Kickstarter projects as they do now? Maybe the creator of Rubbee got lucky? Or maybe he just did everything properly: he presented a unique product, made a list of suitable journalists, and created an intriguing subject and content in each letter?

This story just shows us that there is no secret sauce—everyone finds their own way to success. By the way, Gediminas launched his second Kickstarter project Rubbee X four years later, in 2017. As he had already established contact with press during his first project, this helped to get media attention for the second project, as the press loves follow up stories on something they've covered before and that have achieved significant growth or improvement since then.

Find the Email Address of Any Professional

Based on the BuzzStream survey, 81% want to receive pitches by email. Since this is the best way of communicating, we will discuss how to find the email of the right person.

In some cases, it is published publicly, and news portals have it in the profile of the journalist, along with links to their social media accounts. If this information is not present, find the journalist's personal blog (if they have one) or profile on Twitter (which is often used by journalists) and see if they have contacts listed there. You can immediately start following the journalist and showing them your attention.

So far we have discussed the easiest way, which does not require a lot of effort or knowledge. But if you cannot find their email, you can use various tools that will help you find it. You may simply enter "email finder" to Google and you'll find many options, such as hunter.io, voilanorbert.com, anymailfinder.com, headreach.com, toofr.com, and similar. You may also check other platforms that allow you to verify if the email is correct by entering "email verifier" or "email checker" into Google. Email verifiers (hunter.io, email-checker.net, verify-email.org, etc.) usually allow to verify some emails free of charge, but if you want to do this on a higher scale, you should subscribe to a paid plan.

If you use Gmail you can also try the Chrome extension Sales Navigator for Gmail, and is meant to find person's LinkedIn profile based on their email. After having entered several emails into the addressee field and clicked on every one of them, you will see if some of them match the person's email in their LinkedIn profile. If so, on the right side of Gmail, you will see their LinkedIn profile.

Writing an Email Pitch to Journalists

When writing an email, a strong subject line is a must for a successful outreach. It is especially important because the subject determines if your email will be opened or not. The subject has to be concise, clear, and accurate. To make it more compelling, you may use a keyword related to the topic that is relevant to your product and is covered by the journalist. Once you've drafted a subject line, you may enter it into Strikethrough Headline Analyzer which measures the sentiment of a headline, the likelihood of engagement, and provides an overall score.

Remember that your email will appear in the midst of many others, which the journalist will quickly read, so try to make it simple for them and prepare the content so it will be evident what you want. Imagine that the journalist checks their email on their way to work on the subway, so try to formulate the main question of the letter in such a way that they could answer with only a couple of words. The content should be short, clear, and as personalized as possible. Use the journalist's name and explain why your story is relevant to them, based on their past articles. Before sending the letter, check there are no errors.

It is best to send the email in the morning of recipient's time zone on Tuesdays, Wednesdays, or Thursdays. Avoid sending an email on Mondays when journalists are crowded with information after the weekend, and on Fridays when they are tying up loose ends rather than starting on a new story pitch.

Next, I will provide several successful examples. These letters were sent to journalists who published articles about the discussed topic later on.

This letter was sent to Lulu Chang, who is a writer for Digital Trends:

> Hi Lulu!
>
> I've been following your posts at Digital Trends for a while - great work! As a part of your work is related to digital life influence on humans, I thought this story would be relevant for one of your future articles.
>
> Many people want to enjoy a morning smoothie, but quite often this moment is ruined because noisy blenders wake up their spouse, kids or even angry neighbors! We thought this should stop and developed Millo, the most silent and convenient blender to help those who want to live healthy and keep track of their health progress.
>
> We're planning to launch a Kickstarter campaign for Millo at the end April.
>
> Would you be interested to share our story with your readers?
>
> P.S. You can read more about Millo in our website or watch videos on Facebook.

I used this email to pitch journalists about the smart blender Millo. Since one of the unique features of Millo is that it works much more quietly than other blenders on the market, I decided to catch journalists' attention with that exact fact. The noise emitted by the blender is the most important factor when you want to make a healthy smoothie early in the morning, but you do not want to wake up your spouse or children. That was the problem, which I wanted to emphasize in the subject of this particular email (the subject was "Morning smoothie that doesn't wake up your spouse or kids").

My email started with giving a credit to the journalist and saying a few nice words about her work. Even though recognition of a person's work usually evokes positive emotions, you may choose to skip this and go straight to the point. I wanted to show the journalist that I know which topics she covers and how this relates to the story that I want to pitch. In the second paragraph, I described the problem and the product in short. Then I mentioned that timing is important ("planning to launch <...> at the end April") and finished with a question to encourage her to reply.

Finally I think that a very important line, which people often miss, is the post scriptum or "P.S." In my case, I added more information about Millo, but in general it's a common practice to add links to the press release, product photos, and videos in one folder, so the journalist can get access to everything they need if they decide to write an article.

The response from Lulu Chang came back immediately, after no more than an hour. She replied: "Happy to check out a press release!" As you can see, her response was only a couple of words, but she had showed an interest. After I sent her the press release, she published an article that showed up on Digital Trends in a couple of days.

The next example is for a more niche product. I worked with a startup named Ovao, which was developing a device for swimmers that provides real-time coaching while giving intuitive color-coded instructions on swimming goggles. My goal was to pitch a swimming blog so they would publish an article about Ovao. At that time, only the prototype was ready and since portals did not want to write about this, we decided to create an article for swimmers and give it away for free to one of the portals. After my research, I found 10 portals that wrote about swimming in English. I found contacts of relevant journalists, editors, or blog owners, and sent them personalized emails. Out of ten people, eight replied. This was a great result because usually 3–8% of journalists answer. I think that I received more answers because of several reasons:

- I wrote only to ten people, since there are not a lot of portals that write about swimming in English. If there were a hundred or a thousand portals, I'm sure my response rate would be closer to an average.
- I only wrote to niche websites who publish articles about swimming and receive a lot fewer requests than the big news portals, so the chance to receive an answer is higher.
- I personalized the subject as well as the content, so the recipients understood that a person wrote the letter and it was not some automated email blast.
- I created value—I sent a ready-to-use article on

the relevant topic.

We did not write the article ourselves—we just took a topic relevant to the Ovao product ("The importance of heart rate monitoring for swimmers"), reviewed several articles, created the structure of the content, and hired a freelance copywriter to prepare the article. This is the letter I sent to Brent Rutemiller, the editor of the Swimming World Magazine portal:

> Hi Brent,
>
> I bumped across your articles in Swimming World Magazine. The reason I'm contacting you is because you are truly one of the most influential people in the swimming world and I'd like to hear your feedback on some interesting swimming-related info that I have.
>
> Recently my colleagues at Ovao interviewed a few swimmers who are monitoring their heart rate. Results have shown that most of them use wrist wear trackers (it would be interesting to hear your opinion!) and struggle with them because it's inconvenient to check the device while making strokes and it's a bit complicated to see clearly, especially when goggles are misty. So we started to work on a solution - an eyewear device that displays color-coded heart rate information in swimming goggles in real time.
>
> I've noticed that there are no updated articles on how to boost swimming performance by real-time heart rate monitoring.
>
> I'd like to hear your opinion if such article could be a good fit for Swimming World Magazine?
>
> Waiting for your feedback!
>
> P.S. To make it easier we've prepared a 1000-word text that you (or your colleagues) could adjust or change (depending on your style) and images for this article.

The beginning of this email is similar to the first example. I showed that I knew whom I was writing to, complimented him, and told him that I would like to hear his opinion. In the second paragraph I briefly described how I was related to swimming, explained the problem that Ovao solves, and gave more information about the product. Then I mentioned how outdated search engine results are on articles explaining how to increase swimming results by measuring heart rate. That's a problem for readers who are interested in this topic and an opportunity for portals like Swimming World Magazine to write an updated article and attract new visitors. Finally, I asked if, in his opinion, an article about this would be appropriate for his portal, and informed him that I had one ready. With this, I wanted to emphasize that most of his work was done. I received an answer in a couple of hours.

> We are always interested in articles on heart rate as it relates to training. We can review your article, if you want to send to us.

Then, all that was left to do was to send the text and after some time, the article was published on the Swimming World Magazine portal.

The last example belongs to Mike Del Ponte, the co-founder of the Soma water filter project, which raised more than $100,000 in 10 days. This letter was sent to the editor of the Gear Patrol portal, which was introduced to Mike by his friend.

Hi John

It's great to meet you. I'm a huge fan of Gear Patrol and wanted to pass on something new that could be a nice fit for your kitchen section. I've attached an image of the Soma glass carafe and our revolutionary water filter. Our Kickstarter page has a video and bullet points on why Soma is unique.

We think Soma could be a great story for Gear Patrol for these reasons:

Innovative gear—Soma is the world's first compostable water filter: made of Malaysian coconut shells, vegan silk, and food-based plastic.

Sleek design—The Soma carafe is made of decanter-quality glass, in a world of plastic pitchers. The hour-glass shape is unprecedented in the industry.

Made for busy guys—Soma delivers your water filters right to your door so you never forget when to change it.

If you're interested, please let me know how I can make the writing process easy for your team. I'm happy to send more hi-res photos. We launch Tuesday at 8am PST.

Thanks for taking the time to check us out,

Mike

In all three examples, the text is split into several parts. First, you contact the person using their name, show that you are interested in their work (you know what they write about, what is relevant to them), and that you have information useful to them. Then, a short introduction: who you are, what you do, what kind of problem your product solves, in what way it is unique, what it is for, and why it should be important to the journalist you are writing to. At the end, you should indicate what you need from that person and why the time is important.

As you may have noticed, in all the examples I've shared, journalists were contacted about just a product prototype and were presented only with the idea of it. As the products weren't ready yet, it was a bit risky to share news about it. In this scenario, some journalists may refuse to write about products that are not yet available on the market. In such cases, they may ask to be contacted again when the product is on sale. Others, before writing an article, want to make sure that the product is well made and ask to be sent a sample product. If the quality satisfies them, then they can spread objective information about a tested product. Providing a free product sample is probably the best way to establish a connection with a journalist or other influential person. We'll cover this in more detail in the next chapter.

As I have already mentioned, journalists with a higher authority get hundreds of pitches every day, so it is normal that only a few percent will reply. If you do not get a positive or negative answer, be persistent and send a few more follow up emails. Keep in mind that there is a fine line between being persistent and being annoying, and it is up to you to find that right balance of how many follow-ups to send.

If you have many journalists in your list, use some tools (Yesware, Reply, Mixmax, Boomerang, Streak) that help you automatically send emails at a certain time and monitor how many letters were opened, how many links were clicked, etc. Upon seeing that your letter is currently being read, you can immediately send another email, because the recipient is thinking about it at that particular moment. This will increase your chances of receiving an answer. It often happens that a journalist does not answer, but writes the article anyway. This is fairly normal, since they have a lot of work and cannot report to everyone about the publishing of the article, simply because of time constraints. Use Google Alerts or another tool to get an alert once something that contains your brand name is indexed in Google.

Creating a Press Kit

If journalists are interested in your idea and it seems appropriate to them to publish an article, you will need a press kit, also known as a media kit. This is a package of resources and information provided to journalists to brief them about your product. I suggest storing press kit files on your website (yourwebsite.com/presskit) or in a shared DropBox, Google Drive, or OneDrive folder.

There are no strict rules on creating press kits that specify what components you must include. It will vary based on your product, but there should be at least two main items: high-resolution product photos and the press release. In addition, you may add videos (explaining how your product works, etc.), a fact sheet, technical product specifications, company background, quotes, product brochures, etc. I would recommend making the media kit as simple as possible, because the more items you include, the more work you're making journalists do. The best press kits make it really easy for journalists to quickly learn about the product, and access photos and other materials they can use.

The press release is made up of several parts: headline, introduction, more details about the news, descriptions of company activities and contact information. The headline, similar to an email subject, decides if the reader will want to read the text further. But in this case, the journalist is already interested in the news, so the headline is not so important. In the introduction, summarize the news in two or three sentences, by presenting the most important information. Then reveal more details: what kind of product it is, why it is important, what problem it helps to solve, how it is unique, etc. You can provide facts about the product and the team, and quotes from your co-founders or yourself.

Try to not overdo the press release. Where it is possible, include links to a photo gallery, instructions, videos, and other information, so the reader who wants to find out more can check the appropriate sources. At the end, briefly outline what the company does and leave your contact details. A 400–500-word press release should fit onto one page. To have a better understanding what other creators put in their press release, I suggest taking a look at a few crowdfunding projects that have received more publicity in the media.

PR Agencies and Press Release Distribution Services

Creating a list of suitable journalists, finding their email addresses, and trying to get in touch with them takes time and effort. Is there a more efficient way?

If you have money, you can hire a PR firm that will do this for you. Just make sure they have experience with crowdfunding projects. In the next chapter, I'll share a story about Food Sniffer, that first hired a traditional PR firm which didn't bring any results, and later switched to a smaller PR agency that specialized in crowdfunding projects. With their help, they managed to get huge publicity and were covered in NBC, CNBC, The Daily News, The Financial Times, USA Today, The New York Times, Channel 4, etc.

True PR is *earned* and *never guaranteed* because journalists or editors must *validate your story,* and if it's worth their attention, they *control the final version* of the article. You can hire a PR agency, but even they can't give you a guarantee, because they are just one of the participants in the chain which includes you, the agency, the journalists, and the editors. The journalist may like your topic, but if Donald Trump posts a scandalous tweet on Twitter, Apple presents a new iPhone model, or a thousand other events that are more important than yours happen, your story may not even appear. You should know the risks related to PR (in the worst case scenario, you'll spend money or time or both and no one will write about you) and have reasonable expectations. If you decide to hire a PR agency, determine possible scenarios ("what if...") and discuss them in advance. Some agencies are more flexible and may agree to charge you based on results, or will agree to work on a revenue-sharing model.

Unfortunately, not all of us have the money to hire a

professional PR firm. In this case, entrepreneurs who don't have enough money and don't want to build a media list and contact them one by one, try to look for other alternatives. And sometimes they find press release distribution platforms, such as PRLog.org, PR.com, PR-Inside.com, Newswire.com, OnlinePRNews.com, PRNewswire.com, PRWeb.com, and BusinessWire.com. Such platforms can be free or paid, and prices vary from $99 to $1000 (when choosing the best plan). Here, you can send your message to tens or hundreds of portals in one shot.

Nevertheless, such platforms cannot guarantee the same results that you would reach by creating a *relevant media list* and contacting journalists yourself. One of the reasons is that these platforms are more oriented to the mainstream media, which will hardly be interested in your news—unless, after having presented your project, you receive an offer from Google or Amazon to purchase your startup for a million dollars. You have more chances to interest niche portals, which are read by your target audience. Press release distribution platforms usually skip such portals, so it is best to contact them directly. Whatever the case, press release distribution platforms are worth considering only if PR services have the lowest priority in your to-do list, and if you don't have money to hire a PR firm or don't have time to gather information about relevant journalists or bloggers.

Free Articles vs Paid Articles

Up to this point, we have discussed how to contact journalists and interest them in your idea, so they write an article about you *for free*. Why should they do that? Because news portals earn money from advertising by creating relevant content and they always need new and interesting stories.

If you present your idea to a journalist from the proper angle, they may publish an article, which may bring traffic to your crowdfunding project, and some of the visitors may decide to back your project. In the end, all involved parties are happy: the reader reads an interesting article, the portal earns money from advertising, the journalists receive a source for an article, and you get some publicity and free traffic for your project. But not all projects are interesting enough to be written about by media outlets, and many startups' attempts to present their idea disappear in the journalists' inbox. You can never be sure that they will write about you.

Is there a way to get a *guarantee* that your project will be covered in Forbes or Huffington Post? If you have money, you can buy such a service, which is offered by freelance writers who publish their work on authoritative portals. Some media outlets, when trying to separate these journalists' content from the portal staffs' content, add a note next to their articles that this is a *guest post* or that the person who wrote this article is a *contributor*.

After having browsed some freelancer sites, you will find various offers to write an article in portals like Forbes, TechCrunch, Entrepreneur, Wired, or Mashable. Such a service is paid and you can be sure that the article about your product will be written and if not, you will not have to pay. The price depends on a few factors:

- Portal authority (the higher the domain authority, the higher the price);
- The nature of the article;
- Whether there be a link to your website or not;
- How quick you want the article to be published.

For example, a 500-word article on Forbes may cost about $1,000. If your goal is to collect potential clients, it is more effective to spend these funds on Facebook advertising—it will have a higher return on investment than mentioning your project in a Forbes article. I've spoken to Evan Varsamis, founder and CEO of Gadget Flow about this and he told it's not worth doing, unless it's a homepage article from a reporter (not a guest author or a contributor).

For most people, the fact that a well-known portal such as Forbes wrote about you gives more trust and adds credibility for what you do. Is it necessary? I do not think so, because you can try other, more cost-effective methods to build social proof (by sending free product samples, collecting testimonials, etc.). However, it's good to know that such an option exists, and if you ever decide to get a guaranteed entry in an influential portal, even before presenting your project, consider this as one of the alternatives.

INFLUENCERS

Influencers can be journalists, bloggers, sport or entertainment stars, associations, organizations, the leaders in their area, experts, social media giants who have lots of followers, or any other people who have a smaller or larger audience and create value for their followers or charm them in some way. Influencers have an audience and can drive traffic to your project. That's why influencer outreach is a powerful way to extend your reach with a target audience without relying on traditional media.

Let's say you arrange with an influencer who has tens or hundreds of thousands of followers who match your target audience that they will inform their fans about your project when your campaign starts. What kind of influence might that have on the results of your project? What if you manage to arrange with an organization that has millions of followers?

A perfect illustration in this case is the story of PARKIS. An influencer called Viral Thread took their video, edited it, and shared on their Facebook feed (see picture below) with 15 million followers. The video gathered nearly 25 million views on Facebook! This determined the success of the PARKIS campaign on the Kickstarter platform. So we'll discuss how to encourage organizations or people who have large audiences to share the video or news about your campaign.

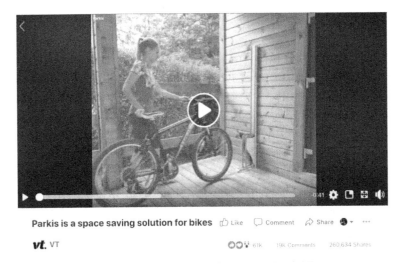

Fig. 35. PARKIS video on the Viral Thread Facebook profile

How to Find Influencers

If you want some influencers to share your project, the best way to do this is by finding people who have already shared something similar. In the previous chapters, we've already discussed possible ways of analyzing crowdfunding campaigns that have some commonality with your project. This is one of the best ways to find influencers whom you could approach. You can do a search from a project by image, keyword, project name, or hashtag (if the project has one) in social networks, or just use specialized tools to find influencers in your niche.

After you've found influencers who have shared similar project to yours, you can do wider research by using certain keywords, such as "top [your niche] influencers" or "key [your niche] influencers." While browsing, you will find various catalogs and tools that will help you in your search:

- **Onalytica** (http://www.onalytica.com). Provides influencer identification, relationship management, and measures influence to better automate and streamline influencing activity and identify engagement opportunities. They also provide influencer lists of different categories in their blog.
- **GroupHigh** (https://www.grouphigh.com). Offers a possibility to build, evaluate, and manage influencer-marketing relationships. You can identify new influencers, organize, and nurture relationships with influencers and report and track earned media from blogs and social media.
- **BuzzSumo** (https://buzzsumo.com). We already discussed it when we reviewed media outreach. This tool helps in finding the most shared content by keyword, identifying influencers in your category, and filtering by location, reach, engagement, and authority.
- **Sprout Social** (https://sproutsocial.com). Helps enhance conversations to let brands easily engage with influencers and build lasting relationships. Keep track of social conversations, customize the way your team uses the platform to facilitate ongoing collaboration, and manage publishing calendars.
- **BuzzStream** (https://www.buzzstream.com). Helps to research influencers, manage your relationships, and conduct outreach that's personalized and efficient.
- **Followerwonk** (https://followerwonk.com). Helps you dig deeper into Twitter analytics. You

can search bios and connect, compare Twitter accounts, segment your followers, compare your relationships with competitors and friends, and match your activities to your followers to give them what they like the most.
- **Traackr** (http://www.traackr.com). Lets you manage, validate, and organize your influencer data in one place, foster team collaboration by assigning ownership, track conversations, and benchmark your brand's influence in the market.

All of the above tools are paid, but they offer free trial, so try them out and evaluate if they are worth your attention. If you want to get more useful platforms that help to find and connect influencers, you can download a complete list of tools here: https://www.kickstarterbook.com/#bonus.

After finding the relevant influencers, you should review them so that you know who is worth contacting. Choose only those whose audience match up with yours and may be interested in your project. Then sort them by reach and engagement. If you are using a special tool, apply some filters, offered by the platform. E.g. BuzzSumo allows sorting the influencers by reach, authority, influence, and engagement. Once you've completed your research and identified which influencers are relevant, you should collect their information (name, email, social handles) and organize them in a spreadsheet.

How to Establish a Connection

Now, as you have a list of relevant contacts ready, you can move on to the next step. Keep in mind that the information you've collected is publicly available on searches, so influencers receive many requests from people every day. When we talked about media outreach, I mentioned that the more authoritative the journalist is, the more pitches they receive. The same rule applies to influencers. So, it is best to start from those influencers who are small enough to be interested in you and large enough to provide benefit to you by posting about your project. The small ones (micro influencers) receive far fewer requests, so the chance to establish a connection is much higher.

After having chosen the suitable people, start following them on social media. Social media platforms often send notifications once someone starts following another person (unless the influencer has turned this off), so this a good first step to get an influencer's attention. If you have a Twitter account, create a special list of influencers, and add the appropriate person to them. After you do that, they will also receive a notification about this. Before contacting an influencer, it's good practice to engage with them. You can do this by liking a few posts or photos and leaving your comment on something they share. This will bring value for the influencer because if their post attracts more likes and comments, this increases their engagement rate.

Then you can establish first contact—just say hello, and give them a compliment or a reason why their profile interests you. For example, on Twitter, you could write: *"Hi @Name, I'm a big fan of your work, looking forward to reading more of your tweets!"* Just as in real life, you should not start presenting your project immediately, and the same goes in social media; you should start with a non-binding greeting and show of respect.

Then, depending on how much time you have, you can either show more interest in the content they share by liking and commenting on it, or you can write your pitch. Usually, the best way to do the outreach is by email, as this has the highest response rate, but you may also use social media platforms. Try different channels and see what works best for you. Personalize your message, make a compliment, introduce yourself, and explain why you have reached out, how your product can benefit them, and what you need from them. You may also try a shorter version: personalize, introduce, and go straight to the point.

Here's a pitch by Ernest, creator of Tealure tea. This message was used to reach out to Instagram influencers:

> Hi {name}
>
> I'm following your blog which is a great source of information and inspiration.
>
> We are about to launch a Kickstarter campaign to introduce one of the most talented tea makers in Nepal, whose teas rarely reach international tea drinkers. Our aim to expose this talented farmer and introduce four unique teas to international tea drinkers. Would you be interested in giving a shout out in return for some teas?:)
>
> Let's have a common goal and promote the remote tea community in Nepal.

Ernest had a list of just seven influencers to whom he sent this message. He received two responses. The first influencer wanted to try out the tea first before sharing the project with his followers, but the Tealure team didn't have tea samples back then. Another answer was much more useful because this particular influencer had covered similar campaigns in the past and agreed to share Tealure's project in his newsletter (this is just another example showing the importance of similar campaign analysis and reaching out to the most relevant people). As a result, this newsletter was seen by one of the biggest tea figures in America, who then shared the Tealure project with his Instagram followers.

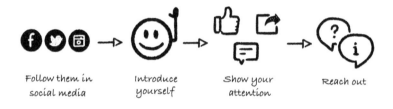

Fig. 36. An example of how to reach out to an influencer

Offer Product Samples or Do the Presentation of the Prototype

In Tealure's example, Ernest offered his product sample in return for a shout out on social networks. This is the best way to interest an influencer. When they have the option to touch, look at, and test out your product, it is much easier for them to form an option and decide if it's worth sharing with others. Of course, this is not applicable in all cases, but if your product is ready-to-use and the self-cost of it is small, you should certainly offer free samples.

However, if you develop a technological product, you may have just one or two prototypes. Moreover, they are especially valuable because they are used for testing purposes, their self-cost is usually big, the design is pretty unsightly, there is no user manual, and they may work with some errors. To send such a prototype to someone is certainly not worth it. It will not leave a positive impression and some problems may arise when testing it, which may ruin your reputation. So it is better if you present a prototype personally and explain how the product works. Only by physically being there with a person who will review your product can you ensure that everything will go smoothly, and that you will minimize all other risks that could happen if you are not present.

Food Sniffer: How to Get onto the Big TV Shows Having Just a Prototype

Talking about a prototype-stage product presentation, I'd like to share the story of Food Sniffer. This is the world's first handheld mobile device that determines the quality, freshness, and safety of meat, poultry, and fish. When this project (the original name was Peres, but it was soon changed to Food Sniffer) was launched, the team had just a prototype. They decided to spread the word with the help of professionals and hired a leading PR agency from London that specialized in health and medical devices. It was expected that after this agency distributed the press release, Food Sniffer would appear on TV and newspapers would write about it. However, none of this happened—it seems that the traditional PR approach just didn't work. Twenty thousand dollars spent on this PR agency didn't bring any results and there was zero user traction for the crowdfunding campaign.

But the Food Sniffer team didn't give up and decided to hire another agency from Florida (PR Media Now), which specialized in crowdfunding campaigns. This time, both parties agreed to work on a revenue-sharing model. This new agency managed to get in touch with journalists, and even though they were interested, their answer was the same: "It's a really interesting gadget, but we can talk about it only once we see it working." So the Food Sniffer team bought tickets and flew to the USA to present their product and give interviews that were arranged by their PR agency.

This worked, and on the last week of their crowdfunding campaign, Food Sniffer was covered in NBC, CNBC, The Daily News, The Financial Times, USA Today, The New York Times, Channel 4, etc. August, one of co-founders of Food Sniffer, said that while they were in the USA Today editorial office, during the presentation, their prototype didn't work and sensors didn't show that the meat wasn't fresh. But this didn't confuse the Food Sniffer team, and they decided to pour some vodka on the meat just to show that their prototype worked! The strangest thing was that this didn't even surprise the journalists of USA Today, and they were absolutely fine with that experiment! It's the perfect example, showing what influence you may have when you present a product yourself.

Finally, during the last 4–5 days of the Food Sniffer campaign, they managed to achieve the biggest success and received $1,000 funding every hour. At the end of their campaign, they had raised $77,556 and we can only guess what funding they could have received if they had arranged all those interviews on day one. It seems like a success story, but what if Augustas hadn't hired another agency? Most probably, he would have ended up with huge losses. The story always has two sides, and you should consider the risks and evaluate what would happen if things hadn't worked out.

Follow Up

Influencers are generally very busy people (that's how they have become influential) and they have their own priorities. It is normal if only a few of them reply to you. So, don't take this personally and follow up again few more times. Be persistent, but don't become annoying and be respectful of their time. If they don't respond after a few messages, stop contacting them, unless that influencer is particularly important for you in the long term.

Paid Posts

With the rising popularity of influencer marketing, many may not agree to share your project in exchange for a free product. Such influencers are more likely to appreciate a straightforward, business-like offer. Ask what they would charge for a shout out. Compare various offers and decide if it is worth investing in it.

If you are afraid that this influencer may take your money and avoid providing the service, you can use an influencer marketing platform that stands between brands (creators) and influencers. In this case, you'll have to pay some commissions for the platform.

VIRAL VIDEOS

A viral video is a video that becomes popular through a viral process of sharing through social media, YouTube, email, or other channels. Such videos spread quickly and attract a large audience.

Many creators normally encourage their friends to share their post about a project launch, but posts never spread as fast as pictures or video footage on social media, since videos are much more attractive to the user. I have already mentioned the PARKIS campaign, during which a viral video, shared by Viral Thread, attracted massive traffic. It was a pleasant surprise for the creators of PARKIS because they did not initiate this process. The Viral Thread agency found their video, edited it, and shared it with their audience.

The video of the Millo smart blender also went viral and gathered more than a half million views after it was shared by Mashable (see Fig. 37 below). Unfortunately, this happened only after the campaign on Kickstarter had ended. We can only guess how things would have turned out if the video clip could have been shared by Mashable during the campaign.

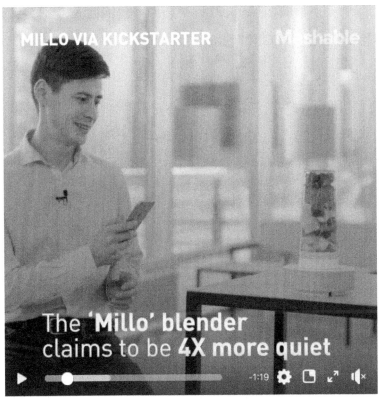

Fig. 37. Millo customized viral video, shared by Mashable

The creators of Paperscope (a postcard that transforms into a kaleidoscope) also had a similar experience—UNILAD Tech shared their edited video clip after their Kickstarter campaign had ended. This video got more than a thousand likes and was shared almost 300 times on Facebook.

Fig. 38. Paperscope customized viral video, shared by UNILAD Tech

In these instances, the project creators didn't submit their video to those portals by themselves. This has happened without their knowledge. But I wouldn't recommend leaving anything to accidental success. There's still plenty you can do to increase your video's chances of becoming viral.

First, make a list of companies that share viral videos. Some of them are: LADbible, UNILAD, Viral Thread, 5-Minute Crafts, Mashable, The Dodo, Food Network, Jake Boys, BuzzFeed Tasty. Most publishers specialize in specific fields, e.g. the BuzzFeed Tasty network specializes in food. Choose companies that are related to your niche. You can find them in search engines by entering keywords like "Top Facebook Video Publishers," "Top 10 Video Creators," etc. or on social networks.

Next, get familiarized with the rules of video publishers. They usually ask you to contact them via email or to fill out a special form. Since the publisher is going to additionally edit your video, give them what they need to work with: unedited (raw) video without text, which will be different from the video you publish on your Kickstarter page. The video should be short—about a minute or two longs. You can also upload a few video clips so they have something to choose from.

That's exactly what the Rubbee team did before they launched their second campaign on Kickstarter. They already had a list of video publishers that might be interested in their video, and shared the raw material with them. As a result, they were chosen by Mashable, who shared a customized Rubbee video which then received 18,000 likes, more than 1,000 comments, and over 17,000 shares.

Fig. 39. Rubbee customized viral video, shared by Mashable

Keep in mind that the biggest video publishers receive thousands of videos every day and in addition to this, they actively search for relevant content. So, the chance that they will share your video is not very big. But if you make a relevant publishers list, prepare raw videos, and submit all this information in advance, you can rest easy, knowing that you have done everything that you could have done.

Another option is to pay for the sharing of your video and be 100% sure that your video will be posted. The situation with *free* and *paid* viral videos is similar to paid articles that we've discussed previously (by default, PR is *free* and *earned*, but there are still options to *get published* for a *certain amount of money*). You have to compare publishing costs and possible results with other paid advertising options and evaluate if it's worth investing. The cost of sharing videos depends on the publisher, the size of their audience, and the engagement level. You will have to negotiate price individually.

WRAP UP AND ACTION PLAN

You may start this action plan as soon as you have developed the idea or, even better, have created a prototype and know that your product has a product/market fit. The essence of the action plan seems simple: you need to spread the message of your idea and attract potential backers, and when you start the project, they should be converted to real backers as soon as possible. But in reality, this process is not easy and requires a lot of preparation, testing, and analysis. Therefore, you are committed to devoting time and effort to the success of your goal.

Gather a Team

If you run a personal project with a relatively small goal, you can work alone. But if you want to achieve something bigger, you will need a team, so start gathering it in advance. If you need a temporary team just for your crowdfunding project, you may invite students for an internship to do simple tasks. For everything else that requires certain skills, hire freelancers.

Set Your Financial Goal Low

Your funding goal should be low, but realistic. Set the

minimum amount you need to make what you have promised and to fulfill all rewards. Calculate your manufacturing, packaging, shipping, and marketing budgets. Don't forget to take into account the Kickstarter platform fee, credit card processing charges, and taxes. Double check whether the estimated profit is sufficient. Once you've launched the project on Kickstarter, you will no longer be able to adjust the goal.

Analyze Similar Campaigns

After searching for similar campaigns, carefully observe their videos, descriptions, rewards, social network profiles, and website (or landing page). Look at what blogs and media outlets have covered these campaigns, what people and in which social networks have shared each project, and where the most traffic came from. Analyze the campaigns' financing graphs in Kicktraq: on which days did they gather the most money, and when did the campaigns receive the biggest number of backers? Finally, get in touch with the authors of these projects, chat with them, and get answers to the main questions.

Define Your Target Audience

After analyzing similar campaigns, you'll already know a bit about your target audience from the "Community" tab, which reveals the top cities and countries of a particular Kickstarter campaign. Even though you can't be 100% sure who your ideal clients are, you can run some A/B tests with Facebook ads and learn more about your target audience's gender, age, income, location, and interests.

Build a List of Your Personal and Business Contacts

Contact your friends and business partners and ask if they want to be notified by email once your project is launched. Remember that every acquaintance can be useful, so try to reach out to everyone and build your mailing list with people who have agreed to be informed about your project.

Create a Landing Page

A landing page will help you automate the lead generation process. Run A/B tests on your squeeze page with different eye-catching visual elements, and find out which one gives better conversion rates. Insert at least two forms (at the top and bottom) to collect contacts. Use an exit intent pop-up form, which will encourage a visitor leaving the site to leave their contact details. When designing your site, make sure that it is mobile-friendly. With Facebook ads, it's cheaper to reach mobile users than desktop users. Make sure that the text, images, and forms are displayed well on different devices. Create a Google Analytics profile and upload a tracking code (tracking ID) to your site to monitor the traffic and conversions.

Link Your Landing Page to an Email Automation Platform

Each contact made on your website has to be automatically moved to your mailing list. If there's no direct integration between your site and email program, you can use Zapier, which allows to automated processes easily.

You already have one mailing list for your personal and business contacts, so create a new mailing list in your email program for leads generated on your landing page. Some email programs require a *double opt-in*, meaning that the visitor who has left their contact details receives an extra email and should click the confirmation link to be added to your mailing list. This ensures a higher quality on your mailing list, but due to the longer procedure, you may lose some leads. People (especially those who are using mobile devices) often tend to be lazy and do not open their email to click the confirmation link. So if available, I suggest using a *single opt-in*.

Prepare a Series of Emails

Create a series of a few automated emails, which will be periodically sent to people who have left their email address on your landing page. The goal of these letters is to "warm up" your leads, to get them engaged, and to make them interested in your project. To improve their engagement, at the end of the email, encourage them to perform a certain action: answer a question, click a link, express their opinion, complete a survey, etc. Monitor your email statistics: what percentage of the people who received that letter open it, click a link, or respond to you?

Create an Account for Facebook Ads

If you plan to collect leads with the help of advertising, the most effective tool is Facebook. Set up Facebook

Pixel, which measures your visitors' actions and helps to build audiences. Activate retargeting for everyone who visits your site. This will make your ads more efficient. People will think that your ads "follow" them wherever they go. It may appear crazy, but this can increase your ad performance several times. Facebook Pixel collects data about your website visitors and once you have a source audience with at least 100 people from a single country, you can create a lookalike audience. Then Facebook will identify the common qualities of those people (e.g. interests or demographic data) and will find people who are similar to (or "look like") them.

Use Other Methods to Collect Leads

There are many methods discussed in this book for gathering potential backers. The earlier you start this, the bigger the audience you will have. Experiment and observe what works and what does not. When possible, incorporate these people into the development process of the project. By doing this, you will increase their engagement. Keep in mind that only a few percent of the people you have gathered will back your project. Remember, it is always better to think of conversion in a pessimistic way. Calculate how many leads you need to collect to reach at least 30% of your goal within the first 48 hours. Collecting those leads should be your top priority during the pre-launch.

Make a List of Journalists and Influencers

Here, the rule of "the sooner the better" also applies. Make a list of journalists and influential people who are relevant to what you do. Start establishing relations with them in advance. The best time to contact journalists with your pitch is around one week before your project launch, once you have a project preview page (we'll talk about that later). If you have a test version (free sample) of your product that you can share with influencers—do that.

Support a Few Projects

This is not necessary, but by doing this, you will show that you actively support other projects and this will provide a certain degree of trust for some backers.

Prepare for the Stagnation Period

Most Kickstarter projects have a funding curve that has a tendency to repeat. Usually, there's one spike at the beginning and another at the end. The first spike shows that creator did their homework and collected a community of potential backers. They were informed about the project in advance and acted immediately to collect the early bird rewards. During the last 48 hours, there's another spike because the deadline is getting close, and Kickstarter sends a reminder for those backers who didn't back the project, but did click the "Remind me" button. The creator also reminds people in their mailing list that it's the last chance to back the project, so the remaining potential backers, who were still considering whether to back the project or not, get it together and back the project in the last days.

But the project takes around 30 days, so it is a hard

task to maintain interest throughout the whole period. That's why you should be ready beforehand. Prepare information and material that will interest your audience and encourage them to back your project. Think about new rewards and stretch goals in advance. Check how creators of other projects engage with their backers throughout the campaign.

STARTING A PROJECT

Kickstarter is a place where you can raise money for your project and build a community around your work. So far, we've covered the pre-launch, which I consider the most important part of a crowdfunding campaign. Nevertheless, your project headline, description, visualizations, and video are very important too, as your project page determines how well the visitors that you bring to your campaign convert to backers.

If you are new to Kickstarter, first you'll need to create your profile in the platform: add your photo, name, a bio, and links to your website and social media profiles. Then, the first step to start a new project is to choose the category. As mentioned earlier, there are 15 project categories on Kickstarter: Art, Comics, Crafts, Dance, Design, Fashion, Film & Video, Food, Games, Journalism, Music, Photography, Publishing, Technology, and Theater.

Choose the one that is the best fit for your project and briefly describe your project idea. You'll be able to update the category and edit the brief description (short blurb) later if something changes. We'll review those fields in the section "Step 2: Project Image, Title, and Funding Goal."

Kickstarter has its rules and project guidelines that you must follow. If you can meet the platform's requirements, then to be able to present your campaign on

Kickstarter, you will have to upload a video and a main picture, describe your project, create rewards, and register an account. In this chapter, we will discuss all of these steps in detail. You can complete those steps in any order; it's not necessary to begin with the first one.

STEP 1: YOUR ELIGIBILITY AND PROJECT RULES

Even though Kickstarter is open to backers all over the world, project creation is currently available only to individuals who are from certain countries and meet the platform requirements.

The first and the main requirement to be able to start a project on Kickstarter is to be a permanent resident of the US, the UK, Canada, Australia, New Zealand, the Netherlands, Denmark, Ireland, Norway, Sweden, Germany, France, Spain, Italy, Austria, Belgium, Switzerland, Luxembourg, Hong Kong, Singapore, Mexico, or Japan. Kickstarter does add new countries to their list, but this process is very slow. So individuals who live in countries that are not allowed by the platform should try some other methods to be accepted (we'll talk about them more in this section).

The second requirement is to be 18 years of age or older. People under the age of 18 can launch projects only in collaboration with an adult or guardian who meets Kickstarter's requirements. The adult will need to verify their identity, enter their banking information in the project build, and assume the responsibilities for fulfillment of the project.

Third, you should have an address, bank account, and government-issued ID based in the country that you're creating a project in. You can create a project in your own name, or on behalf of a registered legal entity with which you are affiliated. If the project is registered to an individual, the linked bank account must belong to the person who verified their identity for your project (in this section, we'll review cases where projects are registered to one person and identity confirmation is done with another). Citizens of the EU (European Union) are welcome to use a government-issued ID from any EU country. But the project must be run in an EU country that is eligible on Kickstarter. Finally, you must have a major credit or debit card.

What if Your Country Isn't on Kickstarter's List?

If your country is accepted by Kickstarter, the account verification process becomes very simple and you may skip this section. But if you are not a permanent resident of one of the eligible countries, this may be one of your biggest headaches. However, it's still possible to launch a campaign. Just it requires a bit more time and effort.

There are few workarounds that you can use. Project creators I interviewed (and I personally) used these methods and they actually work. But please note that none of the information below constitutes legal or tax advice and this is also against Kickstarter's rules. I recommend consulting an attorney and tax accountant before proceeding. You should take full responsibility and use this information at your own risk. If you are not a permanent resident of an eligible country and don't want to take risks or consult a professional, then choose another platform.

The first option is to register the campaign in the name of a person living in one of the accepted countries. It should be a trustworthy person: a relative, a friend, or a business partner. The bank account tied to the campaign on the Kickstarter platform should also belong to that person. You'll need an address, and a scanned passport or government-issued ID to validate this person's identity on Kickstarter. Kickstarter support may ask who this person is, so you'll just have to say that they're a part of your team. It's a normal practice to run a project as a company or group of people, and only one member of the project team who meets Kickstarter eligibility requirements must verify their identity as its representative.

If the project is successful, money will be transferred to this person's bank account, so it's important to know and trust this person, as they will receive your money. I'd recommend consulting with a tax expert to understand what taxes will be applicable for this person and for you. Also keep in mind that if you choose this option, transferring money from Kickstarter to this person's bank account and then from their bank to your bank will take more time and will cost more money, due to bank fees.

This option is appropriate when the funding goal is not too big or if this is a one-time project. That's the option I chose as well. I registered the project on behalf of a business partner in Australia. For this reason, the funds raised for the project were collected in the currency of that country—Australian dollars. I was wondering if maybe this would cause some inconvenience for my backers to support the project, but it seems no one was bothered by this currency.

If you register a campaign in someone else's name, when someone opens your project, they will still see your name on the main project page (created by [your name and surname]). But when they click on your name, the "About the creator" page will pop up and at the bottom, they will see a "check" icon and next to it, the first and last name of the person who has verified their identity and bank account.

Other options I'll mention work if you are an EU (European Union) citizen and have a government-issued ID from any EU country, such as an EU passport or identity card. However, if you are a non-EU citizen, those options may not work. I've interviewed many project creators from the EU who have successfully used one of those methods.

The simplest way is to open a personal bank account in the eligible country. Ignas, creator of Pigeon, had a personal UK bank account from earlier times and it suited him perfectly for a project registration on Kickstarter. Even though Kickstarter requires entering an address in the confirmation process, it seems that they don't verify it. As long as they don't do that, you can enter any address. But their policy may change while you're reading this book. Who knows, maybe in the future they will decide to add more control and ask for a utility bill or other proof to verify your address.

Opening an account in some countries may not be as easy as it seems because banks have strict regulation policies. Therefore, people often look for alternative ways—mobile banking applications. These have a fast registration and verification process and can open you an account several times faster than a regular bank. However, this type of service may not suit Kickstarter, and in the end, you may need to open an account in a real bank. This happened to one of the projects where I was a collaborator. First, we opened a personal account on Revolut and received a GBP account for a non-UK citizen. However, there's one particularity about this type of account...

When someone wants to transfer money to you, they must enter Revolut Ltd as the recipient instead of your first and last name. In addition to that, your identification number should be added, based on which Revolut will know that this specific payment should come to your account. Unfortunately, this is not accepted by Kickstarter as their payment partner, Stripe, does not accept or support non-standard bank accounts, including digital, e-wallet, or cross-border services like Revolut. In order for them to send the funds, they require a standard account (e.g. a checking account) registered with a financial institution based in an accepted country. Keep this in mind because sometimes shortcuts may not work.

Finally, Kickstarter allows creating a project on behalf of a registered legal entity with which you are affiliated. The last option is to open a company and a bank account in an approved country. SPYNDI, the creators of functional furniture, found a subsidiary company of a French bank that "rented" them a French IBAN. That was enough to register a Kickstarter campaign, even though their company was outside approved countries. The SGS Watches team opened a company and bank account in Hong Kong. One particularity about Hong Kong was that they needed to register a local director to open a company. This was rather a formality, but it took some time and effort. Rubbee opened a company and bank account in the United Kingdom with the help of the UK accountancy and professional advisory firm Adams & Moore. You may also try Stripe Atlas platform for forming a company.

Opening a company and a bank account may take more time, but in this case, you'll get all the funding directly. There won't be a need to ask someone for a favor, and think how the income for your friend would be taxed. Choose this option if you expect to raise more funds or if you plan to continue this project after your Kickstarter campaign ends.

Project Rules

If you meet the platform requirements, next, you'll need to review and accept five Kickstarter rules:

1. Projects must create something to share with others.
2. Projects must be honest and clearly presented.
3. Projects can't fundraise for charity.

4. Projects can't offer equity.
5. Projects can't involve prohibited items (drugs, alcohol, nicotine, weapons, political fundraising, etc.

I think all of the rules above are common sense rules. It's all about sharing. Backers make a pledge and in exchange, you give them something you've promised in your reward system.

The second rule also emphasizes that if a project involves manufacturing something complex, like a gadget, Kickstarter requires project creators to show backers a prototype of what they're making. Photorealistic renderings are prohibited. Sometimes, a simple sketch can work better than perfectly created rendering. When I interviewed Ignas, creator of the kick scooter Pigeon that was launched on Kickstarter, I learned that this rule is really strict.

After successfully funding Pigeon on Kickstarter, Ignas was contacted by an investor and together they founded the company Citybirds for creating scooters. After some time, the creator of Pigeon decided to launch a Kickstarter campaign for another kick scooter—Raven. It was the lightest and most compact foldable scooter ever designed by Citybirds. However, when Ignas submitted a project, Kickstarter support responded that the photos they were sharing in their project were "too much rendered" ... Ignas is a designer, so he wanted everything to be perfect, but "too much perfection" in photos was an obstacle to him appearing on Kickstarter. In the end, Ignas decided to choose Indiegogo for Raven because of this limitation.

The third rule is very clear—if you want to raise money for charity, choose another platform that specializes in personal fundraising or causes you care about, such as GoFundMe (https://www.gofundme.com). Even Facebook now has the functionality to create fundraisers and collect donations for your cause directly in the platform (https://www.facebook.com/fundraisers). One interesting story that I'd like to share here happened to Saulius, who decided to create a fundraising campaign to collect money for his studies at the AFI Conservatory in Los Angeles, California. As Kickstarter doesn't allow personal fundraising, he decided to launch his campaign on Indiegogo. He had some friends who had previously raised money for their studies on Indiegogo, so he decided to take the same path. Saulius chose a flexible goal and by the end of his Indiegogo campaign, he had raised over $11,000. And then a strange thing happened... Suddenly he received a message from the platform that all funds raised for his campaign were refunded because personal cause projects are not allowed to run on Indiegogo...

This surprised the creator of the project and all his backers. Sadly, that's a big drawback of Indiegogo, because it doesn't have a project review process (like Kickstarter), which prevents such situations from happening. Hopefully, they will improve their processes in the future, but keep this in mind if you or your friends decide to start a personal fundraising project.

The fourth rule is also similar to the third. If you want

to offer equity, choose an equity-based crowdfunding platform, such as Seedrs or Crowdcube. The fifth rule is quite simple—just make sure that your project and the rewards you want to offer don't include prohibited items, as listed on the Kickstarter page.

Confirm Your Identity and Link a Bank Account

If you meet all the eligibility requirements, it's time to confirm your identity and link a bank account. You'll need to add the contact details and personal details (first and last name, birthday, address, and bank account information) of the recipient of the funds. As discussed previously, the fund recipient can be you, your friend, or the legal entity (company or organization) that you represent. The person whose identity is verified will be displayed publicly on your creator bio.

After filling in all the necessary fields and clicking on the "submit" button, you'll have to wait for some time for an account to be verified. If for some reason Kickstarter is unable to verify your identity through this process, you may be prompted to use an automated system, which will confirm that you have a valid ID, and compare it with an image of your face, as uploaded by you or captured by your webcam. This process is similar to presenting your ID at an airport, except that a machine does the matching, not a human. If there is any trouble with this process, the Kickstarter support team may also step in to help with manually verifying your identity.

Don't be surprised that Kickstarter is taking identity verification so seriously. This process helps to ensure that there is a real person behind every project on Kickstarter and this strengthens the integrity of the platform. It also protects you by preventing someone else from running a project under your name.

STEP 2: PROJECT IMAGE, TITLE, AND FUNDING GOAL

Next you'll have to upload your project's title and image, and set your funding goal and campaign duration. All those items are under the "Basics" tab on the Kickstarter project editing page. In earlier steps, you've already selected a project category and added a short description, so here you'll be able to edit those fields if you want to.

Project Image

This is the first thing that visitors see when they open your project page on Kickstarter. The image has to be high resolution (technical requirements: at least 1024x576 pixels, 16:9 aspect ratio, file limit 200MB, and supported formats are JPEG, PNG, GIF, and BMP), representative of what you're creating, stand out from other projects, accentuate your uniqueness, and prompt interest in a random visitor, so they would like to learn more about your project. Kickstarter recommends providing clean pictures without additional elements (banners, badges, or extra text), so the visitor will not be distracted by excess information.

Project Title

The title of your project should be simple, specific, and memorable. As discussed previously, it should also represent your USP. Choosing a title isn't an easy task because in just a few words, you need to explain what the project is all about, how it is unique, and why it should matter for a random person who has just visited your page. Take a look at the titles of ten successful Kickstarter projects in your category and learn how they differentiate themselves from others.

Keep in mind that Kickstarter's search looks through words from your project title and short blurb (we'll review this next), so make them representative of what you're creating. The words you use in your title will help people find your project not only on Kickstarter, but also in Google, as Kickstarter has a high page rank.

Short Blurb

Here you can add a short description of your project and reveal a bit more detail than in the title. The short blurb has a limit of 135 characters. If you manage to reach a higher ranking in your category or on other Kickstarter search pages ("Recommended for You," "Trending," "Projects We Love," etc.), the short blurb will appear with your project image. Then, if someone clicks on your project, they will see this short description just below your project title.

Category and Subcategory

Here you can edit the category that you chose earlier. You may also choose a subcategory, which is optional, but it allows you to put your product in a certain niche. When a backer wants to explore projects on Kickstarter by category, they can review all projects in that category or only a certain subcategory. If you choose a subcategory, your project will appear under both the subcategory and the parent category. Personally, I think it's worth choosing a subcategory, as you'll give a chance for your project to be found by a backer who narrows down their search as much as possible to find the specific kind of project they want to see.

Project Location

Here you can specify location of your project. It can be any city/country, even if it is not in the list of supported countries. In the Kickstarter search, it's possible to filter projects by broader location (Earth, country, or city) or choose nearby locations.

Funding Goal and Duration

We've already discussed how to set a funding goal in the section "Setting a Goal." The funding duration on Kickstarter can last from 1 to 60 days. Kickstarter has done some research and found that projects lasting any longer are rarely successful. Even though it sounds logical to choose the maximum duration, I wouldn't recommend doing so for two reasons. First, the longer the project lasts, the harder it is to keep the excitement up for your backers. They will simply get bored. Second, if someone backs your project early, they will have a longer timeframe to change their minds and cancel their pledge. I recommend setting your campaign at 25–35 days. Campaigns with shorter durations create a psychological sense of urgency around your project, which results in higher success rates.

Project Collaborators

If you are running your project with a team or with the help of an agency, you may add project collaborators and grant them permissions for your project (edit project, manage community, or fulfillment). Pick collaborators whom you trust because they will be able to see your project data. Collaboration invitations are sent by email and those people must have a Kickstarter account in order to accept your invitation.

STEP 3: PROJECT VIDEO

The video is one of the most important parts of the campaign. Most users prefer to quickly watch a video, rather than reading the project description. Videos are not required to launch the project, but Kickstarter statistics show that campaigns with compelling videos have a double success rate, compared to projects without videos. So why not double the chances of your success?

We've all heard the old marketing rule, which says that "content is king." This may still be true, but nowadays, another important thing to consider is the medium involved. Now video is the new king of content. If you want to attract, interest, and engage potential backers, you will have to dedicate time and resources to get the message across via video.

The video should answer these listed questions in a concise manner:

- What are you planning to make?
- What problem does your product solve?
- How is it unique or different from other alternatives?
- What is your product meant for?
- How can someone use your product?

To keep your viewers' attention, the video should last up to 2 minutes. The first 30 seconds are the most important, since they determine if someone will finish watching the video or turn it off. Once you launch the project, in the creator's dashboard you will see statistics showing how many times the project video was played and what percentage of those plays were completed. If your video is too long, a high percentage of viewers may not watch your video to the end. To grab the viewer's attention and really connect with them, you have to maintain intrigue throughout the video. At the end, there should be an encouragement to act further—to support your project or share it with friends.

You can find inspiration and new ideas by watching videos presented by other Kickstarter creators. Just do not overdo it and do not copy everything. Be yourself: if you feel better when you are serious, be that way, and if you have a great sense of humor, show that. You should convey authentic emotion in your video, so be sincere and vulnerable. Being vulnerable is not a weakness. It's actually a strength because you are not using any kind of a mask to hide the real "you."

Tell your story: what encouraged you to take on this idea? What problem did you encounter? Nowadays, it is said that it's more important *why* you are doing it and not *what* your product does. Daniel Kahneman, who was the first to conceptualize this idea, received a Nobel Prize, so maybe it is worth heeding his advice and conveying your *why*.

For everything to go smoothly, you will have to write a script for the video—what will be said and shown. Rarely will you be able to do it successfully from the first take, so dedicate some time for testing and corrections. Rehearse the speech with your friends—the more often you say it, the better you will do in the final recording of the video. If you do not feel comfortable on camera, you do not have to be filmed. There are a lot of successful videos in which the creators do not even appear.

STEP 4: PROJECT DESCRIPTION

When creating a description, think from the perspective of your target audience. If you were considering buying your own product, what would you want to know before making up your mind? The description should be short and simple, avoid technical jargon, make the text easily readable, and add images: sketches, photos, or other visualizations. If you think that you will not be able to write a good text about the project, give this task to a copywriter.

Visuals are especially important, so provide sketches, images of your prototype, or photos if you have a ready-to-use product. If the product will be in various colors, sizes, or dimensions, list them precisely and understandably. Add user reviews or testimonials, pictures of your team members, GIFs, or a short video, which explains how to use your product.

The structure of the description is usually comprised from several parts. The intro should reflect the essence of the project and its uniqueness. This information has to be presented especially concisely—in one or two sentences. Then describe the problem which your product is meant to solve. Explain why this problem is relevant, why your project should see the light of day, and what it will change. Describe the exceptional features of the product. It would be best to complement this information with facts about the product, the reviews of users, or quotes from the media (if you have that). All of this should help to earn trust and help people to find a reason to support your project.

If your product has a lot of features which you would like to mention, list them. To make the description even more personal, tell your story—how the idea was born, why you set out to implement it, what inspired you. Present facts about yourself, the team, and your experience in this field—the reader should see that you are the best people to bring this idea to life.

In the "Risks and challenges" field, mention the risks which your backers may encounter. Inform them about possible inconveniences (which are usually related to late production and late delivery to backers) and what you will do in these cases.

Seeking transparency, some project creators provide information on how the raised money will be used. This is not mandatory, but could be useful, since potential backers may have such questions. When the project is launched, you will most likely receive many repeating questions. For these purposes, Kickstarter recommends creating a frequently asked questions (FAQ) section. This can be created only after launching the project.

STEP 5: REWARDS AND SHIPPING COSTS

Why do people back projects on crowdfunding platforms? Firstly, they want to be a part of the community that supports creators and encourages them to realize their ideas. But even more important is what backers will receive in exchange for their financial support. That is why you should create motivating rewards for your backers.

Prohibited Items

When creating rewards, you should first look over Kickstarter's prohibited items. The platform doesn't allow anything that is illegal, heavily regulated, or potentially dangerous for backers, as well as rewards that are not directly produced by the creator or the project itself. If you have some doubts about a certain reward that is not in the prohibited list, you can always contact Kickstarter support for clarification.

Reward Description

When setting rewards, you will have to:

- write the title of the reward;
- add a short description (you may also add a list of items included in this reward);
- set the price;
- set the estimated delivery date;
- add shipping details (no shipping involved (for digital products), shipping to certain countries only, or worldwide shipping);
- set the delivery price (you may apply a different price for each country or region);
- set number of units, if the reward is limited (in the case of early bird rewards) or add a start and end date if you want a reward to be available during a certain time period.

The reward title and description should be short and clear. Make a bullet list if the reward consists of a few items. Display reward illustrations in the project's description page, so the backers can see what they will receive. When setting a delivery date, be pessimistic, not optimistic, and add a few extra months to what you have initially planned. Most first-timers on Kickstarter experience delays in creating their product and if they don't deliver on time, they will disappoint their backers and may receive negative reviews and lose their trust. Don't make that mistake and set more pessimistic expectations in advance. If you manage to deliver earlier, you'll just make everyone happy!

Keep in mind that when a backer chooses a certain reward, after you have launched your project, you will not be able to edit it. However, if no one has selected this reward yet, you will be able to make changes or remove it completely. You will also be able create new rewards during the campaign.

Digital and Physical Rewards

Most often, projects are devoted to one specific product, so it is usual to give the finished product or several units of it as a reward. If your product can be both physical and digital (book, movie, song, etc.) offer both options.

I was very happy with digital rewards, because I could send the book in PDF format to my backers very quickly, with minimal expenses and without any problems. But when I was sending the printed books, though, I had to break sweat: sign each book, purchase suitable packaging, calculate the total weight of the package, enter the addresses of all backers into a system, print a list, cut out and attach the backer addresses to the appropriate packages (because each book had a dedication to a specific person), and then fill in customs declarations if the package was going to be sent to a non-EU country.

Additionally, some of the packages never reached their addressee and were returned for various reasons.

So, I had to work quite a bit when sending packages to countries such as Ethiopia, Nigeria, and Kosovo. The shipments were usually returned or, even worse, simply got lost and did not reach their addressee. Although shipment registration and insurance might help to avoid such losses, in my case, it was better to lose a couple of the shipped books, rather than register and insure all shipments. If I could turn back the clock, I would likely have limited project support to certain countries, or I would have registered and insured only those packages that were sent to more risky destinations.

Donation Without a Reward

During the campaign, the rewards are arranged from smallest to largest. The same product may be priced differently, depending on type (digital or physical), unit count (the larger the amount, the lower the price), time (early bird and regular rewards), additional features (if the product will be autographed by you, it can be more expensive), etc. Predicting how much money a stranger will dedicate to your project is very hard. Every backer is different—some can only give a couple of dollars, others several dozen and others several hundred, and there may even be a person willing to donate several thousand.

We already discussed that it is vital to get active backers on the first day. All creators are working hard on their pre-launch strategy, building email lists, outreaching media and influencers, and posting in social media. But there's one group of people who will most probably be your first supporters—your friends and family. But what if the product is not relevant to them? In this case, a symbolic donation is the best choice, since everyone can contribute a couple of dollars without any reward. In this case, the backer picks the sum (usually $1–10) they want to donate to the project. After supporting your project, these people feel a part of the community that brought your dream closer to your goal.

The Kickstarter platform creates these lowest-tier rewards automatically. They will not have any direct influence on your funding goal, since the sums are symbolic, but they will allow you to quickly increase the number of backers. The more backers that support the project in a short time, the bigger the chance that it will appear higher in your category in the Kickstarter search pages. This may attract organic backers who are reviewing projects in a certain category.

Early Bird Rewards

Another type of reward, which is really important for all projects, is an early bird reward. It is a limited amount of your product, offered for a discounted price to the most loyal backers who joined your email list or expressed their interest in your project in another way during your pre-launch campaign. The number of early bird rewards is limited (50, 100, 200 units, or similar) and you can create several levels of them: for example, 50 units for $20—super early bird, 50 units for $25—early bird, etc.

Having a limited number of products for a lower price is a great psychological trigger that will encourage the potential backers you have collected during the pre-launch stage to support the project as early as possible.

Increasing the number of backers and your funding growth are metrics that are used in the Kickstarter popularity algorithm, so if you're able to create a strong launch momentum, this may help attract organic traffic from the platform.

Setting the Reward Price

When setting the price of the product on Kickstarter, creators usually have to sit down and think it over. You should take into account the self-cost of you manufacturing your product, additional expenses that you may experience, and evaluate the market price of alternatives or analogs to your product. If you set the price too high, you are risking receiving not enough support and if you set it too low, the project may not pay back, or you may even experience losses.

Since crowdfunding backers are taking a risk when they support the project and wait for it to be delivered to them, it is normal to set a lower price than the final retail price of the product. For example, if you plan to sell the same product in the future for $100, when presenting the project, sell it for $80–90. When allowing the option to purchase several units of the product, make an appropriate discount, so the backers will be sufficiently motivated to choose this reward.

Also, creatively evaluate the product itself and consider what kind of value you could add. It could be a nicely packaged product, presented as an exceptional gift, a product with your autograph or a personal dedication, a product with certain accessories, etc. By adding more value, you can create additional rewards with a higher price.

The Largest Rewards

The final reward level, which resides at the bottom of the list, is the largest reward. These are usually related to a unique personal experience or something special that the creator can offer.

When I was creating the rewards on Kickstarter for my book *How to Start a VoIP Business*, I estimated that most people would support the project by choosing one unit of the book for $25. Then I calculated that I would need 200 such backers to reach my goal of $5000. After having analyzed other projects related to books, I created more expensive rewards, just in case. One of them was $400 for the option to leave a review on the back cover of the book.

I was shocked when the first supporter not only chose the reward for $400, but donated much more—$500. And that was not even the best news. A day later, another supporter chose the $400 reward, but donated twice as much—$800! Even though this reward was limited to five, there was more demand for it than I had expected initially. Shame that the space on the back cover of the book was limited. And that was not the end of it...

On the fifth day of the project, I was blown away, because one backer bought an excursion in the Old Town of Vilnius for $1,500! The interesting thing is that nothing was included in this reward—this backer from Italy bought flight tickets and paid for accommodation himself. Even when he arrived in Vilnius, I barely managed to convince him to let me pay for lunch, at least...

A similar reward, called "Millo Insider" for £3,000, was created by Adam, the inventor of Millo. Adam was especially happy for having created it. Included in the Millo Insider was not only a Millo blender with accessories, but also a three-day visit to Vilnius, during which the backer would meet the entire Millo team and see the produced prototype. This reward was chosen by one person from the UK, who had saved a significant amount of money and decided to make a change in his life and support young creators who have a great passion for what they do.

When setting a necessary financial goal, evaluate how many units of the project you will have to sell to reach your goal. Don't include the largest rewards in your prediction. It is always better to expect less and be surprised when the campaign takes an unexpected turn. If it so happens that some generous backer chooses that largest available reward, that moment will be one of the most amazing in your life, I have no doubt about it!

STEP 6: PROJECT PREVIEW

While creating a project, you may edit and proofread it dozens of times. Don't be surprised if there are mistakes that you just don't notice, simply because you have looked at the same text too many times. That's why it's good to ask your friends to have a fresh look by providing them a project preview link.

After reviewing your project, they will be able to post their suggestions in a comment field. This way, you will be able to find out important feedback and edit the project. Pay attention to the fact that these comments are public and will be seen by everyone using a project preview link.

The inventor of the Millo blender told me that the best time to contact journalists is when you have a project preview link. During that time, the project is not yet public and they can get access to completely new content which is not yet known to others. By doing this, you can offer journalists an exclusive interview and a possibility to be the first to write about your project.

Once the project is launched, the preview link will be automatically redirected to the live campaign and all comments written by your friends won't be visible.

WRAP-UP AND ACTION PLAN

Complete the Account Verification Process

Before the project is presented, the platform will have to confirm the identity of the person on whose behalf the project is registered. If you are from an eligible country, the account verification process will be fast. If you don't meet Kickstarter's requirements, you may use some workaround, but it will take more time to verify your account. Keep in mind that the platform may notice deficiencies or discrepancies and ask you to refine some information or provide additional documentation.

Create a Video

You can get ideas for the video from other projects. Make a script for your video clip by using adjusted text from your landing page and email sequence. Create a scenario, then select a shooting place and date. At the end of the video, encourage the viewer to back your project.

Describe Your Project

You've already described your project in emails, website, and video. There's no need to reinvent the wheel here. Use the same text with some adjustments to describe your project. Add visual elements, share user reviews, team photos, excerpts from the articles (if you were covered in the media), and other information that will increase your credibility.

Create Rewards

Make them simple and clear. Provide a limited number of early bird rewards to encourage first backers to support your project as soon as the campaign starts. Create bigger rewards for VIP backers. Carefully review your rewards, prices, and shipping fees, as you will not be able to change anything about a specific reward once someone pledges to it.

Submit the Project for Review

After you finish setting up your campaign, you may submit your project for review. Kickstarter recommends allocating at least 2–3 business days for the review process, but on average it's done in 30 hours for most projects.

Get Reviews from Your Friends and Make Adjustments

Once Kickstarter confirms that you are good to go, you can share the project preview link with your friends and colleagues. After getting their feedback, adjust the most important things. Click all the links on your description page to make sure they work. Hire an editor to go over your project page with a close eye for typos.

Get Your Crowd Ready and Send the Press Release

Send personalized emails at least twice (a week and 24 hours before the project launch) to your mailing list. The best time to send the press release to journalists is seven days before launch, once you have the final project preview link. Tell them that they can be the first ones to cover this project. Include the key information, add links to your media kit and share the project preview link. This way, journalists will have all the information needed for an article. When you start the campaign, the project preview link will be automatically redirected to the active project.

LAUNCHING AND RUNNING THE CAMPAIGN

Running the campaign isn't so hard if you've done your pre-launch strategy properly. By now, you should have a list of potential backers, influencers who have tried your product and are ready to share your project with their followers, a list of relevant journalists who have previously written about similar topics, and your family and friends who have agreed to back your project with at least a symbolic donation. If you have that ready, it's time to make a next step—press the "Launch" button.

When you have pressed the "Launch" button, your project will become public and accessible to the entire world. You have sent emails to potential backers and journalists and announced a message to your friends and followers, that *the* day has come and that you need help. So you can better imagine what happens next, we will discuss each step by using the funnel analogy.

Since you have already posted that your campaign has started on various channels, people will find information about your project (see Fig. 40, stage 1). A portion of these people will be interested in your project and after having clicked a link, they will visit your project page (stage 2) and if there is no link, they will find it using Google or the Kickstarter search. By using Google Analytics, in the second stage you can review statistics.

On the campaign page, people skim the description

and usually turn on the video and watch it (stage 3). Not everyone waits till the end of the video, but some of the project page visitors will finish it and decide to press the "Back this project" button (stage 4). After potential backers have picked the most suitable reward, they are asked to enter their credit card data. Now a part of them will start doubting if they really need it. Only the most resolute supporters will enter the necessary information without doubts and, after having pressed the "Pledge" button, become your backers (stage 5).

It's important to note that backers can cancel their pledge anytime before your campaign concludes. That's why I recommend sending a private message through Kickstarter to everyone who has just become your backer. This way, you'll be able to contact them privately again if they decide to cancel their pledge. If you haven't done this, you will lose the opportunity to contact them, find the reason for their cancelation, and provide the right argument to retain their pledge.

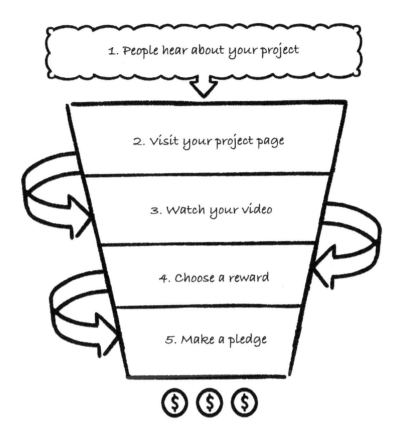

Fig. 40. Process from attracting visitor traffic to the campaign to them supporting the project

PROJECT LAUNCH TIMING

Season

Is your product seasonal? If so, you should launch a crowdfunding campaign in the right season. You can make a small experiment: enter a keyword that describes your product and check it in Google Trends. To give you an example, I've chosen seasonal product—a bike. The Google Trends graph shows that search spikes are in July and the bottom is in December.

Holidays

Timing is also important if you want your backers to get their rewards by a certain event or holiday. Christmas is probably the most popular date. In such instances, you can position your project completely differently—as a special gift for someone. Of course, this can give you additional stress, especially if you are manufacturing something for the first time. Moreover, shipping may be delayed due to higher volumes during the holiday season. So make sure that you leave some buffer room so you can follow through on your promise to deliver rewards before a certain date.

Most people are on holiday during the summer, so June and July aren't ideal months to launch your crowdfunding campaign, unless your product is seasonal and summer is the right time. Also, try to avoid launching in late November, any of December, and the beginning of the New Year. At the end of fall, most are attracted by "Black Friday" and then there's the Christmas holiday period, during which everyone is bombarded by various offers. After the holiday season, people are still recovering from the overspend. Even though you cannot foresee everything, a lot depends on whether the attention of your target audience will not be diverted by more important things.

Day of the Week

If possible, launch your campaign in the middle of a month, when employees get paid, as they feel a bit wealthier on their payday. You can start the project between Tuesday and Thursday (unless it is a big public holiday) —during those days, people are more willing to accept information. Mondays are usually harder, since the workweek starts and people have to catch up on the tasks that have accumulated during the weekend, so they devote less attention to unrelated things. On Friday, people are wrapping up their work and already feeling the weekend. Finally, during the weekend they are resting.

While setting up your campaign, you can set a project length (previously I recommended setting 25–35 days). When choosing the length, keep in mind that Kickstarter has a "Remind Me" button that potential backers can use if they are not ready to back the project yet, but would like to be reminded before the deadline. For such people who clicked this button and haven't backed the project yet, Kickstarter sends an automated reminder 48 hours before the project ends. That's why you may get an influx of backers in the final 48 hours, if many people clicked the "Remind Me" button. Because of this, I'd recommend you end your project on Thursday, so that people get this reminder on Tuesday.

Time of Day

When we discussed media outreach, it was mentioned that the best time to contact journalists is in the morning (their time). The same rule applies here. You should start your project in the morning in your target audience's time zone.

A Helpful Thing to Remember

Remember that the most important thing is how well prepared your campaign is, not when exactly you launch and end your project. If you've done a good pre-launch, you'll most probably have backers to support your project anyway. So, focus all your efforts on the main goal—creating a crowd of fans around your project.

THE LAUNCH DAY

It is probably the most exciting and important day of your campaign. It's the day when your project becomes public and you'll finally see the reaction from your potential backers. Your ultimate goal is to reach 100% funding within 24 hours. However, you should determine this not on the launch day, but during the pre-launch, once you decide how many leads you need to collect.

We've already discussed that you can predict a pessimistic and optimistic conversion rate and calculate what percentage of your goal you may achieve during the first days, with the help of your potential backers. Your minimal target should be around 30% of your funding goal within 48 hours, so if you achieve this or a higher result, you can consider it a good start.

Here's the main list of things you need to do during the first minutes after launching your campaign:

- Send a newsletter to potential backers who opted in to the mailing list.
- Send private messages to your friends, family, and colleagues through the same communication channel that you use with them regularly.
- Email journalists, bloggers, and influencers. Previously, I recommended informing them a week before launch, so this will be your second follow up, confirming that the project is already live.
- Make a post in social media (your personal profile and the project profile) and your blog (if you have one).
- Post to relevant forums, social media groups, and other websites where you've previously engaged with the community during the pre-launch. Don't spam.
- Redirect traffic from your landing page to your Kickstarter page. Before launching, your site has been used to collect leads, and now it should point all site visitors to your campaign.
- Add your pre-written FAQ onto the project page. Kickstarter allows you to add an FAQ only once the project is live, so prepare it in advance and when the time comes, just copy and paste it.

All main tasks should be prepared in advance. You should create the necessary texts, emails, and posts in social media and schedule them. In this case, when your campaign is live, the news about your project will spread automatically and you won't need to worry and stress yourself on the launch day.

In the picture below you can see the financing

statistics of the SGS Watches project. Before starting the campaign, the SGS Watches team collected 4,000 potential backers by using Facebook ads. This helped them to reach their goal within three hours. After 24 hours, they had 173% of their set goal! The result is truly impressive and this again shows how important the pre-launch is. Besides, the more people support your project in as short a time as possible, the bigger the chance that Kickstarter algorithms will place your project higher—thus you will receive a larger user stream from the platform.

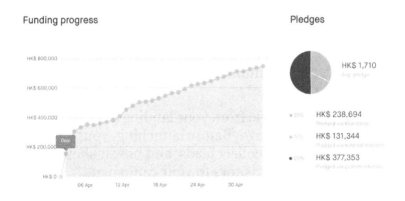

Fig. 41. SGS Watches financing graph

PREPARE TO REFUSE OFFERS

After having started your campaign, hundreds or even thousands of various individual consultants or agencies which offer services to crowdfunding project authors will find out about it. They try to sell their services as soon as you hit the "Launch" button. You will most likely be no exception and will receive a lot of different offers. The target audience of these people is newcomers and project creators who have no previous crowdfunding experience. I would recommend refusing these offers, because when blindly purchasing services of this kind, the results may be disappointing.

Here is one of many letters I received when I started my campaign.

> Hey Vilius, how are you today?
>
> I was about to leave a comment on your Kickstarter's project page but instead I decided to do some research first. Luckily, I was able to find your email so I could reach you directly while there's just enough time.
>
> How would you like to raise some massive support for your project through a highly targeted social media campaign?
>
> If that's something that interests you then give me a call.

This email was personalized with my name and the text was quite compelling, but I knew that general crowdfunding consultants wouldn't be able to help to reach the audience I needed because it was extremely niche.

Sometimes it is hard to refuse such offers, especially if things during your campaign don't go as well as you expected. But I would still suggest you *stick to your plan and keep doing what you have set out to do*. Just ignore all letters and messages of this type.

COMMUNICATION WITH BACKERS

After having launched the project, you will receive emails, messages, and comments from potential and current backers. Review them constantly and reply as quickly as possible. You can also communicate with your Kickstarter audience by posting project updates. It is like a mini blog for the most important events and information related to your project.

Potential backers may wonder whether to support your project or not. Most of them quietly consider this decision in their own thoughts, while just a few will write messages or public comments related to their doubts. That's the perfect chance for you to learn about their concerns and react appropriately. It's especially important to act quickly, while their wish to make a pledge has not yet passed and you can still influence their choice. This rule applies not only when talking to potential backers, but also to everyone else who is interested in your project: journalists, influencers, potential distributors, and other partners. When I interviewed one of the Spyndi representatives, he told that during the Kickstarter campaign, their team worked in shifts to be available 24/7 and quickly react to all inquiries received from different time zones.

If you receive a lot questions, you can optimize the answers by using TextExpander. It allows you to quickly insert "snippets" (email addresses, signatures, text chunks, images, etc.) as you type, using a simple keyboard shortcut, or custom abbreviations. It saves your time without typos and copy/pasting.

You can post a few updates during your campaign and you can select if they will be seen publicly or if only your backers will see them. Here are few ideas for when you can post a comment:

- You reached a significant number of backers (100, 200, 500, etc.).
- Kickstarter mentioned your project in their newsletter or social feed, or selected it as the "Project We Love."
- You raised 50, 100 or 200% of your goal.
- The press covered your project (you can also highlight this in the project description page by mentioning media outlets that wrote about you).
- A well-known influencer shared something interesting about your project.
- You received a great piece of feedback from your backer.

You may also share your excitement during the campaign. People support your project not only to receive their reward—they also feel emotionally attached to what you do, so sharing your emotions shows your vulnerability and creates a stronger bond with your community.

Ask your closest backers who supported your campaign to share their feedback in the comments section of your project. Positive public reviews will increase the credibility of your project.

Prepare some updates in advance: collect unrevealed details, show the first sketches of your product, infographics, statistics, videos, etc. You may also share information about other projects which may be relevant to your backers. Do a favor to other project authors, without asking anything in return. If you are lucky, they will return your favor by doing the same. Creating value in advance is more effective than contacting with a request to cross-promote each other's projects.

Upselling

This is a relatively old sales technique that allows you to make a more profitable deal. By upselling, a seller induces the client to purchase more expensive items, upgrades, or other add-ons. On Kickstarter, a backer can only select one reward and during the campaign, they can upgrade or downgrade their pledge. So, the only way to increase your profit per backer is to encourage upgrading to a more expensive reward.

The first option is upselling within the same reward. If you have the main product and some add-ons to it, you can simply inform your backers that if they want an add-on item, they must increase their pledge by the price of the add-on. For example, your product is a watch and the add-ons are leather straps in different colors that cost $20 per unit. You can inform your backers about this in two ways—private message or an update.

To send a private message, go to your project page, click on "Backer Report," select a backer, and write something like this: "Hi [Name], would you like an additional leather strap in your chosen color? Just add another $20 to your pledge, for every additional strap." At the end of the message, you may add a link for them to edit their reward, which looks like this: https://link_to_your_project/**pledge/edit**). When a backer clicks on this link, they will automatically be directed to the page where they can increase their pledge. You can also inform backers by posting an update, but personalized private messages are more effective. If you have many backers and many choices, after successful funding of your campaign you can try BackerKit to manage your rewards and add-ons.

Another way to upsell something is to create new rewards and encourage backers to choose them instead of their old reward. In this case, take your project link and then add **/pledge/new/** to the end of the link. New rewards are usually introduced with stretch goals.

STRETCH GOALS

In the previous chapters, I have already mentioned that it is recommended to set a low funding goal, but one that is still sufficient to bring your project to life. If you quickly reach 100% funding, the snowball effect will come into play and that will encourage more people to support your campaign. After having reached the primary goal, you can create a stretch goal.

A stretch goal is a new funding target set by the project creator beyond the original Kickstarter goal. The purpose of a stretch goal is to raise more money by encouraging current backers to increase their pledges and share the project with their friends, who can also become new backers of your project. As a creator, you should explain what you promise to do if you reach this goal. In most cases, it is adding more value to your product by introducing new features, add-ons, or other product improvements. You may also unlock more colors, new materials, more sizes, or anything else that makes your product better or more adapted to backers' needs.

It is not enough to just create a stretch goal. You have to actively communicate with your backers via project updates, private messages, emails, and social networks, and encourage them to contribute to the new goal by explaining what additional value they will get in exchange.

After having created stretch goals, upselling to current backers becomes more purposeful, because they not only receive a better product for a relatively small extra fee, but also contribute to realizing something bigger. The real actions of backers will show if your new goal and tactics are effective. In the bottom of the creator dashboard, you'll see all activity related to your project. If you see that backers are adjusting their reward by increasing the pledge amount, your tactic has worked. If they don't increase their pledges, even with your active communication, that means your backers are happy with what they have already chosen and that additional value does not interest them.

Even though a stretch goal is a good strategy in general, as it allows you to raise more money, improve your product, and give your backers additional features they want, it is not suitable for every project. Adding more stuff means that your project will become more complex, new backers may get lost among the variety of rewards, and fulfillment will be more complicated. Manufacturing will also cost more, especially if you outsource it and there's a minimal order. Let's say the manufacturer can produce red leather straps for your watch if you order at least 100 units. If you manage to sell an additional 50 red leather straps with your stretch goal, you'll still have to order 100 units. So, evaluate every aspect, think twice before creating stretch goals, and set the new target responsibly.

GET TRAFFIC FROM KICKSTARTER

Kickstarter has a huge volume of visitors. That's one of the reasons why most creators choose this platform. They expect that at least a small part of organic traffic from Kickstarter will back their project.

Kickstarter has a large variety of options to filter projects for their users: Recommended for You, Projects We Love, Saved Projects, Trending, Nearly Funded, Just Launched, Backed by People You Follow, and Everything. In addition to this, users can select projects in a certain section, category, location, etc. However, while exploring projects, people pay more attention to those campaigns that appear in the first search result page. So the goal of each project creator is to try to keep their campaign as high as possible in Kickstarter's rankings.

Projects that are marked as Projects We Love are determined by a special team on Kickstarter that reviews and selects projects they like, whereas the Trending and Popularity rankings are done by Kickstarter's inner algorithms. The default sort of Advanced Discover search is called "magic." As Kickstarter explains, it displays a rotating cross section of compelling projects by surfacing a mixture of Projects We Love and what's popular.

What Does the Kickstarter Team Say About Organic Traffic?

Even though I would recommend being pessimistic and not to expect any backers from Kickstarter, I was still curious myself to learn if there are some statistics on how many backers came from organic Kickstarter searches. I searched for the answer in the public Kickstarter statistics. Sadly, I did not find the information I was looking for, so I decided to contact the platform's team. I received this answer:

When it comes to getting new backers, we see time and time again that getting the word out through your own existing networks is the most effective. Many people browsing Kickstarter do look around for new projects to back, but the majority of the people who find and back your project will be friends, friends of friends, or fans of the work you do.

It's a very general answer, but Kickstarter states that the majority of backers will be your own crowd and only a small group of people who browse Kickstarter and look around for new projects might support your campaign.

Once your campaign is live, in the project's dashboard you'll be able to see how much money was pledged via Kickstarter. You may think: "That's the number that shows organic traffic!" However, it's not accurate because not all people will back your project instantly after you send them a link. Some of them may need some time to think, some will remember you after a certain time, etc. Even though they knew about your project earlier, whether from you, your ads, or another source, they may later enter your project name in Google or the Kickstarter search, find your campaign, and make a pledge. As a result, such backers will be shown as those who pledged via Kickstarter, even though they originally learned about you from somewhere else.

How Kickstarter Selects "Projects We Love"

There's a dedicated team on Kickstarter that is constantly looking for exceptional projects. They are reviewed manually and those that really stand out as particularly compelling are marked with the "Projects We Love" badge. This is universally considered a good thing because your project then appears higher in default Kickstarter searches, sorted by "magic."

There's no secret recipe for how to get featured in the "Projects We Love," but here are few general tips that you can follow in order to have the best possible chance of catching the eye of the Kickstarter staff:

1. **Start with a strong idea—and express it clearly.** Choose a title which is short and clear. Don't overhype it. Proofread it to make sure your text is free of typos.

2. **Choose a compelling project image.** Make it clear, bright, and simple. Don't cover your images with badges ("Staff pick," "Free Shipping," "Live on Kickstarter," etc.), or other distracting graphics.

3. **Put the most important information first.** Make sure your project description page starts with a short and clear statement about what you're doing. Imagine that someone is skimming just the first two paragraphs. What information would you want them to see?

4. **Illustrate your description and rewards.** Do not limit yourself to text; use high-quality photos, videos, and GIFs in your description. Eye-catching images and GIFs make your story more engaging. Show something related to your creative process: sketches of the first prototype, moments from your life in your studio, etc. When you describe rewards, you can only add text, so show images of your rewards in the project description.

5. **Stay oriented to your target audience and don't spam**. Send emails to those who have expressed their interest in receiving notifications from you. Don't promote your project where it shouldn't be promoted or send unsolicited messages to people you don't know. Whether you're doing it via email or on social networks, it's against Kickstarter's Community Guidelines and could get you suspended from the platform.

6. **Check other "Projects We Love" and subscribe to the Kickstarter newsletter**. This will help you to get an idea of which projects they feature. Most of them will have well-crafted videos, striking images, a clear plan, an excited community, and a lot of creativity. Maybe you'll find some inspiration that you can use for your project.

As you see, those tips aren't something extraordinary.

They just remind you that you actually need to focus on creating an authentic, purpose-driven campaign. Don't expect to be featured or as it's been said, hope for the best but plan for the worst.

Finally, you can write a short story about your project and send an email to stories@kickstarter.com. I suggest sending it not immediately after launching your project, but after a more significant event, such as when your project is noticed by a famous media outlet, your video becomes viral, or you are interviewed about your project on some TV show. If you haven't reached any significant event, just write a short but heartfelt email, emphasizing why your project is important and exceptional. Since those emails are reviewed by Kickstarter staff, honesty and real emotions can influence their decisions.

Will You Attract More Backers if You Get the "Projects We Love" Badge?

I'm sure all creators would love to get this badge. But have you ever considered what effect it will actually have on your campaign? I decided to ask creators who were able to get the "Projects We Love" badge.

The Lava Drops guitar project appeared in the "Projects We Love" category 3–4 days after its launch. Even though the Lava Drops campaign received more traffic, none of it converted to financial support. The author of this project concluded that handcrafted guitars were too much of a niche project and that is why it was not relevant to those who accidentally noticed the campaign. Another reason could be related to the pricing, which started at $2,100 per guitar. So there's a big chance that if you have a niche product, the "Projects We Love" badge may not bring you any backers.

The Paperscope postcard-kaleidoscope is another project that got into the "Projects We Love" category. According to the Paperscope production manager, their team had hoped that they would receive more benefit from getting into this category, but in reality, it barely changed the financial results. As with most campaigns, Paperscope had a spike of backers during the first two days (32 backers on the first day and 30 on the second). The third day number of backers dropped to 13. On the fourth day (similarly to Lava Drops) they got the "Projects We Love" badge, but this barely changed the number of backers—it was 14. On the fifth and sixth day, it dropped to 13 backers per day again. This was very strange because unlike Lava Drops, their audience was very wide—anyone could use a postcard-kaleidoscope and the price was just around $13 for two Paperscopes.

Two examples aren't enough to make accurate comparisons, but it seems that the "Projects We Love" badge doesn't bring significant benefits if you don't appear in the TOP positions of the Kickstarter search or if you are not mentioned in Kickstarter's newsletter or social networks.

Being Featured in Kickstarter's Newsletter and Social Networks

Some of the "Projects We Love" are showcased on the Kickstarter homepage, social networks, and newsletters.

Kickstarter's mailing list has a large group of highly targeted potential backers who may be interested in funding worthy campaigns, even though they have no prior connection to the project.

If you get featured in the platform's newsletter, you'll certainly feel a boost of backers that day. I'm subscribed to the "Projects We Love" newsletter myself and while I was writing this paragraph, I opened the most recent email, reviewed the featured projects, and checked their funding statistics in kicktraq.com. All of them had a spike on that day. However, there's one problem. There are around 4,000 live campaigns on Kickstarter, and on average, four projects are featured in a weekly "Projects We Love" newsletter. So the chances of being selected are very low.

Kickstarter also features some projects in social network posts: Facebook, Twitter, YouTube (but they usually don't promote projects there), and Instagram. I compared the results of the most recent projects that were mentioned on social networks and found that the highest engagement is achieved in Instagram. Post performance on Facebook and Twitter is very similar, but significantly lower than Instagram. However, Instagram doesn't allow the adding of clickable links to posts (unless you buy ads), so even though engagement is high, the conversion rate is relatively low compared to newsletters.

Popularity Algorithm

If you choose "Trending" projects on Kickstarter, they are sorted by "Popularity," which is another algorithm that creators try to hack. Kickstarter does not reveal this algorithm and its dynamics (how often it refreshes in the search) for obvious reasons. However, there are a few known factors that influence the rankings of specific projects.

An investigation performed by Prefundia shows that the most heavily weighted metric within this algorithm is number of backers per day. Suppose there are two identical projects and the first one has ten backers who pledged \$100 each (total amount 10*100 = \$1,000) and the other project has received one pledge of \$1,000. The first one will get a higher "Popularity" ranking because even though the raised amount was the same, it attracted more backers in the same period. According to Prefundia, the percent funded and total amount raised are the next drivers, though their impact is significantly less weighty.

Another metric, which may influence the "Popularity" algorithm, is traffic volume to a project page within a certain time and traffic conversion rate (the better it converts, the higher the project appears in the Kickstarter search). Even though I cannot guarantee this is true, it does make sense—Kickstarter earns commissions from all successful projects, so it's in their interest to attract new visitors and get the best possible conversion rate.

What conclusions can we make here? Nothing new—just follow all suggestions in the previous chapters: prepare the mailing list of your potential backers, establish relations with influencers, pitch journalists, and perform other actions that may bring people to your campaign. Now you know that every backer counts, so don't forget to encourage your friends and family to support your project with at least a $1 pledge on day one. Everything else will be out of your control. If you appear higher in your category—great. If not—there's no need to worry.

What Happens if You Appear Higher in Your Category?

We've already discussed that even if you are selected for the "Projects We Love," this fact itself doesn't give you extra traffic. You should either be mentioned in the Kickstarter's newsletter, social networks, or appear higher in the platform's search.

If you appear in Kickstarter's newsletter, you'll certainly get at an increase of backers, but just for that one day. If you are mentioned on the platform's social channels, there's a chance that you'll get some additional traffic, but conversion will be lower than from the newsletter. Finally, if you appear higher in your category, the traffic you get will depend on your position and how long you are able to maintain it. I think this can bring the most backers, but it's also the most difficult to achieve.

All the creators I interviewed who managed to appear in the Top 20 in their category received extra backers from Kickstarter. But the story that I heard from the Spyndi representative was the most mysterious one. According to the Kickstarter statistics (as mentioned before, it's not very accurate), 37% of Spyndi's campaign backers came from the platform. The first week the organic traffic was good, but the second week it started decreasing, because new projects appeared in the same category and pushed Spyndi to lower positions. Then a strange thing happened. They received a message with an offer to promote Spyndi's project and get it into the Top 20 in the Design category and keep this position for the rest of campaign. Even though first it sounded like a scam, the Spyndi team decided to make a risk and take this offer. And it worked—for the remaining time of the campaign, they remained in the Top 20 in the Design category.

I asked Spyndi to share the contact details of this company and I visited their website. Their site didn't look very professional and I didn't find more feedback about them from other creators, so I decided not to share this information in my book. But if you understand the possible risks and are curious about their services, you can contact me by email vilius.stanislovaitis@gmail.com and I'll point you to their website. You may find more offers to improve your Kickstarter project rank in Google, but in general, my suggestion is to be extremely careful with such services.

LAST DAYS OF YOUR PROJECT

The last days of your project are the last chance to get those backers who were interested, but delayed their decision for different reasons. It's very important that your project is fully funded by that time because seeing "100% funded" and a number of backers who have already provided their support makes it more compelling for others to back your project.

As mentioned before, 48 hours before the end of the campaign, Kickstarter automatically sends an email to those who pressed the "Remind me" button, but haven't backed the project yet. You won't know how many people actually pressed that button, but some of them may also be leads in your list. My suggestion is to send one email before the Kickstarter reminder and one after. E.g. 60 hours and 24 hours before the end of your project. You can also add a countdown timer (if your newsletter program supports this feature) in your email, which will create additional urgency.

Even though a simple reminder will work well, you can still be more creative. Earlier, we discussed stretch goals. Why not introduce an exclusive reward 60 hours before your project ends? This would inspire a rush of pledge upgrades and new pledges. You can send personalized messages (go to "View Backer Report" in your dashboard and select "Message Backers") for your backers who have chosen a lower reward tier and encourage them to upgrade. Creating a stretch goal at the end of the campaign may sound like a higher risk for the creator, but this can be a great strategy because time limitation is one of the most powerful buying triggers. If you prepare everything in advance and create realistic stretch goals, those 60 hours may be long enough to get this extra funding.

Finally, schedule posts in social media in advance (when 48, 24, 12, 6, and 2 hours are left). You may use Canva to easily create attractive and appropriately sized images for such posts. Make your last project update. Express your gratitude for all who have shared and backed your project and make this final request to support your campaign.

WRAP-UP AND ACTION PLAN

You can start executing this plan once your project is launched.

Add a Google Analytics Tracking ID to Your Project

It's extremely important to understand how your promotion efforts are paying off, and where backers are finding your project. To do that, you should enter your Google Analytics tracking ID in your Kickstarter project settings. Google Analytics provides extensive breakdowns of referrer data, gives insights about the traffic to your project page, shows conversion rates, and more. To track traffic more efficiently, create a new filter to exclude visits from your collaborators and you.

Inform All the People Who Agreed to Be Notified by Email

Send personalized emails to all of your friends, acquaintances, potential backers, and influencers—everyone who has opted in to your mailing list or agreed to be informed about your project in other way.

Send a Press Release to Journalists

You can send the press release in advance (when there is a week, or a day or two before the start of the project) or for immediate release. Keep in mind that when the campaign starts, everyone will have access to the project, so you can interest journalists by giving them a preview link so they can get acquainted with the project. By doing this, you will give them an exclusive opportunity to be the first to write about your project.

Update Your Links

Redirect your website visitors to your project and add the appropriate link to your social network profiles, email signature, and other channels.

Make an Announcement in Social Media

Make a post in social media (your personal profile and the project profile) and your blog (if you have one). Post to relevant forums, social media groups, and other websites where you've previously engaged with the community during the pre-launch. Don't spam.

Launch Remarketing Campaign and Run Ads

If you have previously installed Facebook Pixel and created a Custom Audience for your website visitors, launch a remarketing campaign once your project is live. This time, redirect the visitors to your Kickstarter campaign.

The biggest networks for remarketing are Facebook and Google, so if you use Google Ads, you may also launch a remarketing campaign on the Google network. Remarketing is a proven method that will make your ads more efficient. You may run a remarketing campaign for 3-5 days and then pause it, so that you don't overwhelm people.

During pre-launch, your ad goal was to collect leads (email addresses), but once the campaign is live, your goal is to generate new pledges. Try different ad sets with a smaller budget to get a better understanding of what works and what doesn't. Pick the combination of text, images, and audience that has the best performance. Select top 3–5 ads and increase your budget for them. Stop other low-performance campaigns.

Add FAQ

Add your pre-written FAQ onto the project page. Kickstarter allows you to add an FAQ only once the project is live, so prepare it in advance and when time comes, just copy and paste it.

Be Responsive

Constantly review emails, comments, and private messages on Kickstarter and other inquiries from people interested in your work. Reply to them as quickly as possible.

Analyze Which Channels Perform Better

On the platform, you will see the number of backers and what channel they came from. You will also be able to identify additional channels that gave positive results, by using custom referral tags. For a more detailed analysis, use Google Analytics. Monitor what works best, and then devote your attention to that.

If you run ads, conversions will be hard to track. Lots of people who see your ad may open a new tab, go to your Kickstarter page or Google, and search for your project. In this case, you won't see that those actions were originally influenced by your ads.

Reach 30% of Your Goal Within 48 Hours

Crowdfunding platforms highly value successful projects. One of the success factors is how fast you reach your goal. The actions you've taken during the pre-launch will determine how much money will be raised within 48 hours. But not everything depends on your actions—there's also the factor of luck that plays a role too. Hope for the best, plan for the worst.

During the Campaign, Write a Few Updates

It is best to publish them after a significant event. If, in the first 48 hours, you reach 20–30% of your goal, thank your first backers. After you reach 50% of the goal, inform everyone that you are halfway to your goal, and encourage the rest to back the project. After reaching your goal, celebrate together. A well-known portal wrote about you? Make sure to indicate that on the campaign description—that will provide additional trust in your project.

Stay in Contact with Your Audience Via Email and Social Networks

A newsletter is the most effective method to communicate with your potential backers. Be persistent when trying to get them to back your project, but do not overstep the line. Also, share relevant news and the progress of your project on social networks.

Create Stretch Goals and Upsell

Plan your stretch goals in advance. You can introduce them after you meet your original goal or before the end of your campaign. Upsell your rewards through project updates, direct messages, and personalized emails. Analyze when your backers adjust their pledges and work out which methods work better than others.

Schedule Reminders and Posts in Social Media

Automate emails and posts in social media that are related with timing (60, 48, 24 hours left, etc.). In this way, potential backers will get the message at the right moment and you'll use your time more efficiently.

FULFILLMENT

A crowdfunding campaign is a small but important step in your idea realization process. If you succeed in reaching your goal, congratulations! Say thank you to everyone who helped and contributed to your project, share your excitement with others, and take a moment to celebrate this with your team! Then get ready, because this is where the difficult phase starts—delivering what you have promised.

Receiving the Funds

As mentioned before, when the backer chooses a reward and enters their credit card details, the platform only stores this information, but does not withdraw the money. Kickstarter starts charging credit cards only if the goal is reached and after the campaign has ended.

For various reasons, some of the credit cards may not be processed and you may lose some pledges. If a payment cannot be collected, the platform sends emails to such backers with instructions to fix their pledge and follows up with periodic reminders every 48 hours throughout the following week. You can also go to your "Backer Report," sort it by "Errored pledges" and message those backers if you'd like to be involved in this process too. Backers will have 7 days from the end of the project to fix their payments. After the end of this period, Kickstarter will try again to collect pledges, but if this second attempt also fails, such pledges will be dropped.

The pledge collection process takes 14 days and then Kickstarter sends a report, which gives detailed information about gross and dropped pledges, refunds, the platform fee, payment processing fee, and final payment amount. The payout will be transferred to the bank account which you provided during project registration. Depending on the intermediary banks involved in the transfer process, you may need to wait for an additional 3–14 business days for the funds to reach your account.

The last project I collaborated in received £13,927 gross pledges and of these, £2,420 were dropped... That was more than 17% of the total funding! I was expecting that we could lose up to 10% due to different problems related to credit card processing, but 17% of dropped pledges really shocked me. Anyway, you can't predict everything. From the remaining amount of £11,507, Kickstarter deducted a 5% platform fee (£575.35) and around 3% (£355.75) for the payment processing, which left us with £10,575.90.

TAXES

In most cases, funds raised on Kickstarter are considered income. It is taxed differently depending on where you live. I recommend consulting with a local tax advisor and finding out what taxes you'll have to pay.

SURVEY

Once you know the final list of backers whose payment went through, you can start creating a survey to collect necessary information: shipping addresses, sizes, colors, materials of your product, or anything else related to your rewards.

You can send a survey through Kickstarter only once, so think through all the questions in advance. As fulfillment takes time, you may allow backers to change their shipping addresses until you're ready to actually ship rewards. Once you're ready to ship, you'll need to indicate this on Kickstarter and backers will receive a notification that they have 48 hours to enter their final addresses.

A simple survey can be done on the Kickstarter platform, but if you have a complex reward structure with many choices and there are many backers, you may consider using a fulfillment partner. Kickstarter lists trusted companies on their site.

COMMUNICATION WITH YOUR BACKERS

You should continue communication with your backers through updates, keeping them in the loop and informing them about the progress of your project. Since the Kickstarter community has many first-time creators, backers tend to be more tolerant when it comes to late deliveries. But if you realize that you will not be able to keep to your promises to deliver by the estimated date, notify your backers as soon as possible. Post the project update and explain the situation. Be honest and open, because these people have contributed to the implementation of your idea.

Spotlight

After successfully funding your project, you will have the opportunity to use the Kickstarter "Spotlight" feature, which allows you to customize your project page. You will be able to edit your description, title, and blurb, change the background (add a solid color or upload an image), upload a new project image, customize the button, and point all page visitors to your new website or anywhere else.

Indiegogo InDemand

Once your Kickstarter campaign ends, you cannot accept new backers there, but you can still continue pre-orders elsewhere until your product is ready for mass production. I suggest selling through your website, although it may take time to get it ready. Another option is to take advantage of Indiegogo's InDemand program, which allows you to continue taking orders from your backers without deadlines or an additional fundraising goal. It's like a bridge between crowdfunding and commerce.

Transition from Kickstarter to Indiegogo InDemand is quite easy. You may contact the Indiegogo team by email indemand@indiegogo.com for more questions. Funds raised in InDemand are disbursed to you every four weeks. Indiegogo takes fees similar to Kickstarter's—a 5% platform fee and around 3% for credit card processing.

AMAZON LAUNCHPAD

Amazon Launchpad is a hub that helps creators launch, market, and distribute their products to hundreds of millions of customers across the globe. It partners with many platforms, including Kickstarter and Indiegogo, so creators who have launched their crowdfunding campaigns can have their products featured on Amazon Launchpad. This program offers retail expertise, comprehensive marketing support, custom product pages, and access to Amazon's global fulfillment network, which will help you to be discovered by new audiences.

WHAT IF FUNDING IS UNSUCCESSFUL?

Failure is the teacher in our path to success. If your project is unsuccessful, try to understand the reasons behind this. Take your time to think this through and write down your conclusions. It's not always easy to understand the core reason for the failure, but it's worth writing your thoughts immediately, whether they are correct or not. We tend to forget things as time goes by, so having notes about our failures and successes makes it easy to access information from which we can learn something.

If your project was fine, but the campaign was unsuccessful, possible failure reasons could be related to your project goal (it was too big), your audience (you didn't collect enough leads during pre-launch, or leads that you attracted didn't match the profile of your ideal customer), and marketing plan (advertising didn't pay back, journalists weren't interested in your pitch, you weren't able to attract any backers from the platform, your product was too niche, etc.). Once you've made necessary improvements, you can always re-launch your project.

One last thing: unsuccessful projects are still accessible through Kickstarter's search, but the platform de-indexes them so they don't show up in external search engines (Google, Bing, etc.).

FINAL POINTS

Crowdfunding is probably the best tool for people who have time and ideas but lack the financial resources to realize them. Earlier, people had to have their own funds and if they did not, they had to borrow from relatives, friends, or acquaintances. If those people did not lend it, the only way was to get credit from financial institutions. Although for more favorable financing conditions, you need a security deposit and without it the sum is limited and the interest increases significantly, when the author of an idea receives financial support on Kickstarter or Indiegogo, they can freely distribute the money, committing only to the people who supported their idea and their project. This creates a trust-based system between the creators and supporters of their idea. The creator can realize their idea in a certain time by using the money collected for pre-orders, and the supporter feels moral satisfaction because they have helped to realize the author's idea. This increases the responsibility of young creators. When they are realizing their ideas for the first time, they are learning the basics of business processes and the supporters can look at the author of the idea not as another salesman but as a person who is willing to sacrifice their time and resources to realize their dream.

So, my wish to everyone who has ideas is to take the first step. No one is too young or too old to start something new. If you have an idea that does not let you sleep at night, then act upon and realize it. You will never regret that. Worst case scenario—you will not be able to reach your goal but you will get priceless experience, receive reviews from real users, and find out what to do differently the next time. Best case scenario—you will receive money with which you will be able to realize your idea, gather connections useful in business, publicity, clients with whom you will have a close-knit relationship, and new skills that you would not be able to learn anywhere else.

I want for you to use the ideas from this book to realize your goals and if you see that there is not enough information or have any questions that have not been mentioned here, do not be afraid to reach out. Good luck!

SHOUT OUT YOUR FEEDBACK

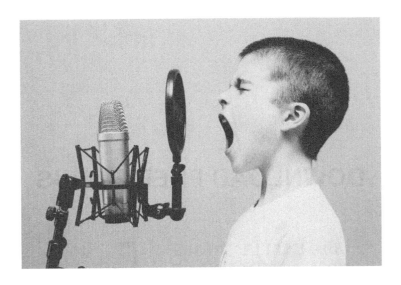

Fig. 42. Photo by Jason Rosewell from Unsplash.com

I hope you enjoyed this book! It would be greatly appreciated if you left an honest review on Amazon. As you know, reader reviews are very useful in making choices whether to read a book or not, so I invite you to add your voice to the mix.

Thanks so much!

- Vilius Stanislovaitis

DOWNLOAD FREE BONUS

150+ USEFUL TOOLS
TO MAXIMISE YOUR
KICKSTARTER CAMPAIGN

Download this Free Bonus to get the most out of this book!

Go to: https://www.kickstarterbook.com/#bonus

ACKNOWLEDGEMENTS

The manuscript of this book was sent to the best crowdfunding experts who have reviewed it and suggested what could be improved. I wish to thank those people for their contribution to this book; Valentí Acconcia, for answering my questions by email (especially keeping in mind that at that time, he was a father of 11 months old baby and was working on 10 crowdfunding campaigns for his clients); Peter Bowles, for sharing the case study about 3Doodler; Miranda Fleming for being the fastest to review the book; Wendy Qi, for supporting the creator community on Kickstarter; Samit Patel, for sharing his "Twitter hack" tips; Daniel Mascarenhas, for sharing his tips on how to improve the title of the book.

Special thanks should be given to Harry Cutler-Smith, who took quite a lot of his time to review this book. Due to Harry's professional experience and valuable information, this book has truly transformed for the better.

I would also like to thank Evan Varsamis, founder and CEO of Gadget Flow for his useful and constructive recommendations on this book.

This book is based on my personal experience and interviews with creators who successfully funded their projects in Kickstarter. I would like to express my very sincere appreciation to all of them for taking the time to answer my questions and share their experience.

Finally, I wish to thank my family and friends for their support and encouragement throughout my journey with this book.

Made in the USA
Middletown, DE
05 November 2020